MW01172814

The Pursuit of Peace

*A Bohemian's Search for Meaning
And Where He Found It*

Book Two of the Believe It or Not Series

by

Max E. Wood

.

Published by
Council Publications
Copyright© 2016 by Max Wood
All rights reserved.

ISBN: 151768739X
ISBN–13: 9781517687397

Also by the same author

The Gates of Hell
*An Atheist's Encounter with the Spirit World
and Where It Led Him*
And Your House
*Salvation is For the Family Not Just the
Individual*
The Drugs and Alcohol Primer
*The Christian's Introduction to the World of
Substance Abuse and Recovery*
Beyond the Smokescreen
*A 10 Day 12-Step Smoking Cessation Pro-
gram*
Rock and Roll an Analysis of the Music
*An Appeal for Readers To Be Aware of What
They Are Listening To.*

Available Soon . . .

What Is Your Name?
*Discover Your Identity and Know What to Do
by Knowing Who You Are*
Through the Beaded Curtain
An Autobiographic Novel
War in the Heavenlies
A Spiritual Warfare Commentary on Ephesians
The Survival Guide for the Spiritual Warrior
Hard-Learned Lessons in Spiritual Warfare

INTRODUCTION

Some do not believe in the existence of a spiritual dimension. I can certainly relate, for I was once of the same opinion. But something happened that created a paradigm shift in me. Through this book I invite you to accompany me on a journey through that *something* and perhaps find insights along the way that will prove beneficial in your own pursuit.

I shall be eternally grateful for the events described herein, for without them my days in this world would have forever remained as flat as a two–dimensional picture. It is the discovery of that third dimension, the spiritual dimension, which gives depth and meaning to life.

But that is not all, for while a more productive and fulfilling life is reason enough to share my story, there is much more at stake than just purpose; more on that later. For now, join me, if you will, on the most meaningful quest of all time: *The Pursuit of Peace*.

Max E. Wood

TABLE OF CONTENTS

DEDICATION

Rev. Bruce Hawthorn is mentioned often in the latter part of this book. If it were not for him, his family and his workers, I would not have this story to tell at all. While he is gone from us now I will forever be indebted to him. What an extraordinary gift he was to us all. For those who knew him at a distance, he was wonder enough but for those of us who knew him best are keenly aware that it is nearly impossible to portray through the medium of words the person that he was. There will never be another. For those who missed the blessing of knowing him altogether suffice it to say that the world is a much better place because of his kind. It is to his memory that I dedicate this book.

CHAPTER 1

VAGRANT PAGANS

The flashing red lights of the police cruiser reflected in the rear-view mirror as the rising sun glared in our eyes. It was about 8:00 AM; and what a night it had been. Somewhere near Erie Pennsylvania we had stopped at a rest area and tried to sleep–but to no avail. Something, we city-slickers were sure that it could have been nothing less than a bear, had come crashing through the thicket next to where we lay on the damp ground. We had all ran screaming to the car. Meanwhile, whatever was in the bushes made its getaway, more terrified of us than we were of it, I am sure. The rest of the night was spent at the Buick Inn. I have hated sleeping in a vehicle ever since.

Now the officer from the cruiser was looking in the driver's window asking for the car's registration, and Liz's driver's license. He returned to the cruiser with the documents in hand. We wondered among ourselves why we were pulled over. Liz had not been speeding or driving erratically. So much for avoiding the turnpike and taking the road less traveled so we wouldn't be stopped by the police. We found out later that Dunkirk, NY was a traffic trap. Soon the officer returned.

"I'm sorry, but I'm going to have to ask you all to step out of the vehicle."

"Why, what's wrong?" Liz asked as we obeyed his order.

"There's a problem with your vehicle's registration," the officer explained. Now that was the last thing any of us expected.

"Who is Max Wood?" he asked looking around the circle of faces.

"That's me," I nervously raised my hand.

"These plates are in your name, but they are for a 1954 Ford."

"Yeah, I know."

"This is a 1956 Buick."

"Yeah," I said, looking at the red and white rag-top, "The Ford didn't even make it home before the drive shaft fell off."

"Well you can't let other people use your plates," the officer explained, "It's against the law."

"But when Rick here," I pointed with my thumb "bought this car, we asked the notary public if I could put my plates on it. He said it was OK."

"So, you own this car?" the officer asked Rick.

"Yes."

"Do you have the title with you?"

"Sure, right over there in the glove compartment," Rick pointed.

"Would you get it please?"

"Yes sir," he sprang into action.

As old as I was, you would have thought that I would have known better than to let someone else use my license plates. But the fact was that I knew nearly nothing when it came to legal matters. When Rick's dad had told us that we needed to go to the Knowta Republic I told him that I just wanted to do some business, not leave the country. As it turns out the notary public had a sick sense of humor—and he didn't like hippies.

Rick returned unfolding the title as he came then handed it over to the officer. Looking at it the officer spoke,

"Rick Rogers. This Buick was titled to you just two weeks ago. The plates are for a 1954 Ford, in His name," he nodded in my direction. "You have an improperly registered vehicle on the road."

"But the notary public . . ." Rick began. The officer cut him off.

"When you let your vehicle be taken out on the road you're responsible for it," he informed Rick.

Holding Liz's driver's license in his hand he turned to her and asked

"And you're Elizabeth Bunner, right?" Liz admitted that she was.

"You've been operating an improperly registered vehicle."

Silence.

"I'm going to have to ask you three to get into the cruiser. We are going to have to impound the car."

The officer then gestured toward, Dave and Al, the two other members of our troupe saying, "You two are free to go."

"Without the car?" Al asked.

"Yes."

"We're from Akron Ohio," Dave protested. "We don't know anyone here. In fact, I don't even know where here is. Where will we go?"

"There's a motel two blocks down the street. It's on the right," he was told.

Soon a tow truck was on the scene and the Buick was taken away down the street. Rick and I were hauled off in the cruiser. A second police car was radioed out for Liz. Rick gave the peace sign to Dave and Al as we pulled away leaving them standing beside the road.

As we rode along, Rick looked at me saying,

"I don't know why police don't go out and chase down the real criminals and leave us law-abiding citizens alone,"

He made sure that it was with sufficient volume for the policeman to hear. The officer replied,

"Well you see, I was just fishing," he glanced back at Rick.

"Fishing?" Rick asked.

"Yes fishing!" the officer repeated himself. He went on to explain. "The number one way we catch criminals is by traffic checks."

"But why did you stop us?" Rick asked.

"Like I said, I was fishing. I was hoping to catch a big one but it looks like I just caught a couple of little suckers," he chuckled.

"Funny!" Rick responded.

After a few minutes of silence, the officer spoke again,

"Actually, I stopped you because you were from out of town, and because of the condition of your car. We have safety inspections here in New York. Your car didn't look like it would pass."

When we got to the police station they took everything we had on us and put it in big manila envelopes. They even took my Bible. We waited in a large room where two adjacent walls were lined with what looked like church pews. This area was sectioned off from the rest of the room by a waist-high partition that had two gates, one on each side of the room, to let people in or out. The rest of the room was filled with desks, swivel chairs, typewriters, and file cabinets. People were busily coming and going while telephones rang incessantly. By now it was 10 o'clock in the morning.

One of the uniformed men from their side of the partition told us to come to the other side of the room where he sat down at a desk with a typewriter and began asking questions. I was first. He typed while I answered, if you can call poking with index fingers typing. As he laboriously filled out the form, there was the standard, name, address, place and date of birth type questions. Then he came up with one that surprised me.

"Religion?" he asked.

"Huh?"

"What's your religion?" he repeated the question.

"Istinity! " I said, using our homebrewed word for our faith.

Our booking agent looked up from his typewriter. Now it was his turn.

"Huh?"

I was used to that response. And I never liked it. I always wished there was a known word that described us.

"Istinity," I repeated, "we're Istinits."

"I never heard of that. What is it?"

"Trust me," I answered. "You don't have time to hear about it right now."

"OK then," He hit an "X" on the typewriter and went on asking questions and pounding the keys with his index fingers.

After being booked we were taken to a large cell, which they called the holding tank. There were nine others in the cell with us —standing room only. And there was one open toilet smack in the middle of the floor. It was a long time before I had to use it.

The men were all sharing stories regarding what they were "in" for. One squat, beady-eyed, large boned, unshaven, red-haired man of about 35 was the loudest. He was there for beating up his wife, which of course he didn't do. He boisterously informed everyone that during an evening of drinking, the effects of which, I could tell, he was still feeling, and through a strange twist of events, it was actually a misunderstanding, she falsely accused him, and it was all her fault anyway. Others began telling their stories. Someone eventually got around to asking us what we were "in" for. After all their extravagant tales I felt intimidated telling them that we were picked up for a traffic violation. I was wishing we had at least knocked off a popsicle stand. No matter though. They all began playing lawyer, offering us advice, and telling us that they couldn't put me in jail for having my plates on the wrong car. After all what if someone had stolen them? Anyway, we were clearly accepted into the fellowship of the cell.

By evening–I suppose it was evening, I couldn't tell since there weren't any windows; all but four of us were disposed of –one way or the other. Sitting on the edge of one of the bunks Rick asked me,

"Why couldn't you sign your plates over to me?"

"That's it!" I yelled.

Immediately grabbing up a Styrofoam cup I began running it across the bars shouting "Turnkey! Turnkey!" I had seen them do that in the movies with metal cups to summon the guards. My cup didn't have the same effect. Styrofoam pieces went flying everywhere. Then Rick and I climbed up the bars to the top of the cell and began jerking them back and forth shouting at the top of our voices,

"Turnkey! Turnkey!"

When one showed up I asked him if I could sign my plates over to Rick. He said I couldn't do that. Once plates are assigned to a person they stay that way.

"Ok! Then, couldn't I just get new plates?" Rick wondered.

Sure, he could, but since the car was titled in the state of Ohio that is where it would have to be done.

Rats! How about, could Rick sign his car over to me, I suggested, and I could get my plates transferred over to it.

Sure, that could be done too–in Ohio. Foiled again!

Not that it really mattered. We didn't have enough money anyway. We had invested most of our cash in gas for the car. All that was left of our pooled resources was about five bucks. What were we thinking?

The officer told us that there was also a towing charge, not to mention an ever increasing impound lot fee.

I was beginning to feel like we were being taken to the cleaners.

Lying down on one of the four bunks for the night I asked Rick what the man processing us had marked down when I told him our religion was Istinity.

"I think he put you down as a pagan," Rick said.

"Pagan?" I sat back up throwing my legs over the edge of the bed. "What's that?" I had never heard the word before despite my obsession with both reading and writing.

"I'm not sure but I know it's a religious term. I think it means that you get your own interpretation out of the Bible," he explained. Rick never was much good at English.

"What? You mean they already have a name for what we are? Then why did we bother making up our own name?"

"Guess no one thought of it at the time."

"Where'd you learn that word anyway?" I asked skeptically.

"From my Dad; he's always working crossword puzzles."

"I'll be! Pagan," I said, half to myself, as I lay back with my hands behind my head. It had been a long and stressful day, and I hadn't gotten much rest the night before. I soon fell into a deep sleep.

I was roused the next morning by a guard running his nightstick along the bars of the cell and calling out "Breakfast!" An effective enough alarm clock. I looked around finding it difficult to believe where I was. Everything had the surrealism of a dream about it. Somewhere between falling asleep and waking they had replenished our cell with more prisoners. The breakfast was good. Best meal I had had for a long time. Eggs, bacon, toast, coffee –the works! I *could get to like this*, I thought to myself. If I can say nothing else for the Dunkirk, New York jail experience, we sure ate well!

As I devoured my meal, I couldn't help wondering how Liz was making out and where Al and Dave had gone.

After breakfast, Rick and I were transported by police cruiser to Mayville, Chautauqua County's seat, for a hearing. We chatted amicably with the officers as we rode through the lush, green, rolling hills of this north shore county. Chautauqua, which is known for its grape arbors and berry farms, and the landscape was in full foliage. The early morning sun lent itself to the bright atmosphere. But the reality was, atmosphere notwithstanding, we were prisoners on our way to a hall of justice.

The courtroom was full when we arrived. There were cases from all over the county present and a number of newspaper reporters. The local press of this ultra-conservative community had already taken notice of our presence in their midst, quickly making us the talk of the county. Native residents had heard about this hippie thing but had never seen any of them first hand. We were a curiosity to them. The first newspaper article about us ran under the heading "West Coast Invades Area". West coast my foot. We were from less than 200 miles to the west of them. I can't imagine what it must have been like for this part of the world when Woodstock struck them a few years later.

On this occasion, I was glad my name started with W. I would be one of the last ones called forward. Rick would break the ice for me. In the end, that did not work in my favor. When summoned, Rick stepped forward. The judge began.

"You have been charged with having an improperly registered vehicle on the road. Would you mind telling me where you were going?"

"To the World's Fair in Montreal," Rick answered in his most respectful tone, adding "your honor" after a pause.

"With five dollars in your pocket?" the judge asked.

The courtroom filled with snickers.

"We had a tank full of gas," Rick responded defensively then added in a somewhat agitated tone, "Before you took our car from us that is!" I rolled my eyes; *Here we go!* Rick never did make much of a hit with authorities. It was kind of a gift with him. The snickers in the courtroom had now turned to mild laughter as the judge looked over the top of his glasses.

"Young man," he said "If you could afford to get your car out of the impound lot, by what I hear it wouldn't likely pass our safety inspection anyway. This is New York, not Ohio! Furthermore, with just five dollars between the five of you, we would just have to arrest you again. We have a law against vagrancy in New York!"

That was all Rick was going to take,

"We are NOT being flagrant!" he screamed. Like I said, Rick never was very good with English.

The whole courtroom broke out in uproarious laughter. People were hooting, and hollering, slapping their knees and stomping the floor.

"We were minding our own business," Rick's voice rose above the confusion, "just driving down the road. You were the ones who stopped us!"

The judge banged his gavel on the desk repeatedly saying, "Order in the court! Order in the court!" The laughter stopped suddenly.

"One more outburst like that, young man, and I'll hold you in contempt of court!" the judge said firmly. "I did not say that we have a law against flagrancy," he went on in staccato speech. "I said vagrancy, with a v! It means not having any money. I'm charging you a $45 dollar fine or thirty days in jail!"

He slammed his gavel on the desk,

"NEXT!" He demanded as if to hurriedly whisk this case out the back door. But, it came back in through the window when he got to me.

"You are charged with improper use of your license plates," The judge announced after calling me forward.

"But the notary public in Ohio said that it was OK," I explained once more. The snickering started again. The judge looked up from his papers and around the courtroom, over the top of his glasses. The snickering stopped immediately. He then looked at me and informed me that maybe it was that way in Ohio but this was New York, so I was being fined $45 or 30 days in jail.

That was it. He was done for the day. I was his last case. But it didn't look like we were going to be done for 30 days. Since neither Rick nor I had the $45 it seemed like a sure thing that we were going to be spending a month in jail.

The next several days were among the most boring in my life. Rick and I were given an exclusive cellblock, on the second floor of the county jail. We had it all to ourselves. No company, no reading material, no TV, only piped in music all day long. I remember hearing *Buffalo Springfield's* "For What It's Worth" over and over again. If I heard "Hey, stop, what's that sound; everybody look what's goin' down" once, I heard it a hundred times that week. Rather ironic, I thought, such an anti-establishment song being piped into a place like this.

At least here we could see out the windows of the hall along our cellblock. The only problem was that they were so high that all you could see was sky. Even at that, daylight was better than what we had in the Dunkirk holding tank.

One big difference between the county jail and the Dunkirk facility was the food. It wasn't nearly as good here as it had been in Dunkirk.

The only thing that kept us from going crazy was acting crazy. Whenever the trustee would bring our meals to us, we would come running out of our cells hunkered over like cave men with our swinging arms dangling to the floor, shouting "Lark! Lark! Grog!!!" then climb up the cell block bars and hanging like monkeys in trees scratching imaginary fleas on our ribs "ooo ooo ah ooo ooo aah aah!" The trustee took a liking to our show and to us. He must have told the cooks about it because the meals began to improve. The trustee later told us that we were getting food that the other inmates weren't. He also began bringing us what we considered far more important than the food—cigarettes, the basic monetary unit of the penal system at the time.

After several days, Rick and I finally broke down and called our parents asking them to send money for our fines. They both said they would, but mine got there first. After saying goodbye to Rick, and while being processed out, the man at the desk said, "Hey, your girlfriend is getting out today too!"

"Really? Where is she being held?" I asked.

"She's here in the same building," he said.

"When will she be released?"

"Within the hour," He said.

I decided to wait. I didn't have anywhere to go anyway. I didn't even know where I was for sure. Besides, I could just see myself getting picked up for vagrancy as soon as I stepped onto the sidewalk in front of the jail. But Liz always had a sense of direction about her. I was sure that together we would come up with a plan to avoid being arrested again.

I took a seat on a bench in the hall. All I had with me was my Bible. I looked down at where it rested on my blue-jeaned leg. Looking up I caught a policeman staring at me with a curious expression on his face. I suppose he had heard about this hippie thing and had been reading about the local invasion in the paper. At that moment, no doubt his preconceived notions about hippies were being challenged, by encountering one with a Bible on his knee. He probably thought that maybe they weren't so bad after all. As he sauntered up to me, I knew that I was about to get my chance to make a good impression. In a most pleasant voice, he asked,

"So, what's your religion?"

I used to wrestle a lot with that question, but no more! I knew what I was now!

"Oh, I'm a pagan!" I said as if I was proud of it.

If ever I saw a wave of shock sweep across someone's face it was right then. The policeman's mouth literally dropped open.

"You're WHAT?" he exclaimed.

Somewhat bewildered I repeated myself,

"I–I said I'm a pagan!"

His brow furrowed,

"Then what in the world are you doing with that Bible?" He demanded.

What was the matter with this man? Didn't he know plain English? Had he never heard the meaning of the word? I thought I'd better help him out.

"Oh, well, uh, that. . . yes, well, you see, I get my own interpretation out of it."

The furrow on the policeman's brow deepened further as his face grew red. Then he asked in an elevated voice through clenched teeth.

"A smart aleck eh? Where are you from?"

I was rattled. My reply was quick but confused,

"Akron, in Ohio . . . I mean . . . I was born in Chicago . . . but . . . "

He cut me off.

"I don't know who raised you, or where, but they sure didn't do a very good job of it!" he bellowed.

I sat there like a toad on a log in a hail storm, with a blank look on my face. Actually, I was scared to say anything. Turning, he stormed down the hall and disappeared into one of the offices. I didn't have a clue as to what went wrong.

"Great!" I thought to myself. "That's all I need, to get the cops in this place mad at me. Now I'm a flagrant vagrant!"

Before long Liz showed up. It was great to see her again. Having not laid eyes upon her for nearly a week I was struck anew by her loveliness. Some people say that beauty is in the eye of the beholder but when it came to Liz the opinion was universal; she was exquisite. At times, I almost felt as if I was in the presence of an angel. Liz was a medium height, graceful, well-proportioned young lady. She usually wore a navy pea coat and often dressed in the latest "mod" clothes. But for now, she wore blue jeans, a pullover shirt, and boots. She carried her pea coat over her arm. Generally, her clothes were wrinkle free with every hair in place. Neat as a pin and clean as a whistle and picture perfect described her well. Her thick black hair was straight and incredibly silky. It hung to the middle of her back, where it was cut evenly across. The front of it was fashioned into bangs that covered her eyebrows stopping just above her blue eyes. The bangs were contoured to fit her face, which was set off by a pair of thin pale lips. Although sweet and kind, Liz had an extreme persona of the mystique. She might have passed for an Egyptian princess had she been more tanned. We all called her Liz but I often referred to her as *The Prophetess* not only because of her cryptic ways but also because of her obsession with the Near Eastern philosopher Kahlil Gibran whose most popular work was entitled *The Prophet*. One thing was for certain, she had an uncanny ability for often knowing what was about to happen just before it did. I highly respected whatever the connection was that she seemed to have with the unknown.

Although I deeply admired Liz's quiet dark temper as well as her physical appearance, our relationship was never anything other than platonic.

After Liz was processed out we walked down the hall, discussing when Rick might be released and the vagrancy law. As we started down the steps to the front door of the building I spied an ashtray with cigarettes stuck into its sand. I stopped and collected a healthy portion of the longer butts.

As I scarfed them up I remembered a friend's father once telling me that if I ever came to a place where I had to choose between buying a pack of cigarettes or a sandwich and I chose the cigarettes I would know that I had sold my soul. I didn't have the money for either right now, but trust me; I wasn't worried about the sandwich. Stepping to the sidewalk in front of the building I immediately lit up the longest butt I had retrieved. I think Liz was disgusted but *hey, this was my habit, not hers.*

"Well, what do we do now?" I asked.

She thought for only a moment then said, "We've got to find the others."

"Fine by me, but we'll have to get to Dunkirk to pick up their trail," I said.

Liz and I didn't have a penny between us. It was Rick who had been carrying our five dollars and it, along with the rest of his belongings, was in a big manila envelope in a file cabinet buried somewhere deep in the heart of the building we were standing in front of. We walked to the edge of town where I stuck out my thumb and tried to hitch a ride. Car after car passed by. I finally gave it up and we just walked along the busy road. After a while, we came to a crossroads where Liz and I got into an argument over which way we should go. She wanted to take the back road. But I wanted to stick to the main route. It just made better sense to go where the cars are if your goal is to get a ride.

"Remember," she said, "I told you guys to stay on the turnpike. But no, you had to take the back road so the police wouldn't stop us. How did that turn out?"

"Well, maybe that was just a coincidence," I suggested although I didn't think so for a minute.

"Do what you will, but I'm not letting you get me to go against my better judgment again. I'm taking this road."

In the end, I grudgingly gave in and went along with her, but was soon convinced that we had indeed made a mistake. This road was dead silent except for the chirping of the birds. We were surrounded by what appeared to be endless miles of berry bushes and there were no cars in sight. The further we walked down that hot, dusty road the more agitated I became.

After several miles, I was about to give Liz a piece of my mind, when off in the distance we heard the roaring of an engine. It was a car! Straining our eyes, we saw it round the top of a hill in the distance, its' chrome gleaming in the sun, and kicking up a trail of dust. It then disappeared into the valley, only to surface again at the top of the next hill.

"This is it!" Liz said in a matter of fact way.

"This is what?" I asked sardonically.

"This is our ride," She said calmly, "that's why we took this road."

We watched while the car plunged into the next valley. When it came up over the top of the next hill it was just a quarter of a mile from us.

"Quick! Stick out your thumb!" Liz pressed. And so I did. The dark blue Mercury came to a halt just before it reached us. A voice from inside said,

"Wow! I can't believe it, guys! It really is them! This is great!"

As we climbed into the back seat of the car I noticed there were three teenage boys in the front seat and one in the back. Before we were even seated the boy who belonged to the voice said from the front seat, "Man, the whole countryside is talking about you guys! It's all over the papers. I can't believe you spoke up to judge Pietro like that!"

"Well, it actually wasn't me," I corrected him, "It was the other guy."

"This is like meeting celebrities," the boy said, "I can't believe you just happened to be walking down this back road."

"According to her," I said, pointing at Liz with my thumb, "We weren't. It was her idea to take this road."

The boy in the middle of the front seat chimed in, "Well we're on it because we don't want to take any chances on getting stopped by the law," It was clear that they had been drinking.

The driver looked over his shoulder at my Bible and asked "Hey! You got a Bible? Cool! What religion are you?"

"Oh, me? I'm a pagan," Liz glanced at me out of the corner of her eye, with a puzzled look.

"Well then, why the Bible?" the driver asked. Now, what was this? Didn't anyone in those parts know the meaning of the word pagan?

"Well I get my own interpretation out of it," I answered.

The boy in the back seat spoke up

"That's OK man! I'm a Lutheran."

"I'm a Catholic!" said the boy in the middle of the front.

What they were, was half drunk–all of them. It made me uneasy, being in a car in the middle of nowhere with four inebriated teenagers and a beautiful girl like Liz. Besides, where we were from most of the time the likes of them didn't take well to hippies. But Liz didn't seem to be a bit alarmed.

I pulled out my next longest cigarette butt and started to light it when the driver asked,

"Hey –you want cigarettes? Joe –give them a cigarette or two."

"Sure thing!" Joe said as he pulled out a pack of Pall Mall's and threw about half of them into the back seat. They landed all over Liz's pea coat. I was rich! Collecting them, I lit one up, and put the rest in my pocket.

"So where are you guys headed?" the driver asked.

"We were going to Dunkirk. We need to find the others who were with us," Liz said.

"Then Dunkirk it is!" announced the driver.

"Good old Dunkirk. That's where you guys got picked up by the police wasn't it?" Joe asked adding, "That place is a traffic trap."

"Did you know, you two were headed the wrong way back there?" asked the fellow in the back.

"We might have gotten turned around, but we wanted to avoid the main road," Liz noted, "I was afraid that we might get picked up for vagrancy."

"Oh, didn't you hear?" said the middle boy in the front. "They repealed that law just yesterday in our state."

"No kidding? They must've seen us coming," I said.

Talk about falling on your feet! A change in a state law just when we needed it most! Of course, the change in the law didn't change what we were. We were still vagrants, which meant we were broke; and we were still pagans. It was just that now both of them were legal.

It was about 2 o'clock in the afternoon when we got into Dunkirk. The boys dropped us off at the Lutheran church because the boy in the back seat had heard that they would help people get a place to stay —so they wouldn't be picked up for vagrancy. Maybe they had helped our friends find a place.

There was a secretary in the church who sent us several blocks down the street to a house the church had bought for office space. There we met the pastor who spied my Bible and wanted to know if I was a child of the faith, whatever that was supposed to mean.

"Oh, I'm a pagan," I said.

I got the same puzzled look from Liz and the same question from the pastor all the others had been asking.

"Well, why are you carrying that Bible then?"

I gave the same answer, only this time in a somewhat irritated tone,

"I get my own interpretation out of it!"

"I see," Was all he said.

Yes, as it turned out, Al and Dave had been there about a week before. They had not been able to help them find a place to stay, but they had been able to get them temporary employment picking raspberries. They had heard several conflicting reports about where they were staying.

It was about five when we left the house. We spent what was left of the day unsuccessfully running down the different leads we had been given. The only report we did not have time to check out was the one about them renting a cheap beach house on the shores of Lake Erie.

We began that night trying to sleep in the cinder block enclosure to a ladies' restroom at a closed gas station. It was very cold that night, especially for the middle of June. It had to be some kind of a record breaker. The enclosure at least gave us shelter from the stiff breeze that was blowing, but it was still cold. Liz found a flag on the premises and insisted that we cover up with it. Again, we ended up in an argument. It was bad enough that we were risking a trespassing charge. Imagine the trouble we'd be in if the police caught us desecrating a flag by using it as a blanket. I was not real excited about going back to jail. In the end, she won the argument, as usual. We sat on the ground in the enclosure with our backs up against the building covered up to our necks with the flag.

As we sat peering long into the dark at the concrete block wall in front of us we fell into conversation and the conversation shortly turned to spiritual matters, which was common for us since Liz claimed to be a spiritual person. Shortly our discussion settled on the subject of inner peace.

". . . well, that's how it is with me Liz," I was saying, "I'm just looking for something that will satisfy."

"How do you mean?" She asked.

"I'm searching for something. But I don't know what it is—or where to find it."

"OK. Could you elaborate a little?"

"Well," I stated. "It's like this cigarette I'm smoking . . ." I held up one of my burning trophies from our afternoon ride, "Do you know what I'm going to do after I'm done with it?"

"What? Put it out?" She guessed in her smart—aleck way. Liz didn't smoke.

"Yeah, but after that, I'm going to light up another one."

"I'm sure you will, everybody else does."

"Right! And I feel ridiculous being controlled by this little white stick. Do you know what these people ask you?" I was getting a little louder.

"What people?" She asked in a whisper, looking around, as if to say, 'Keep it down!'

"The ones who push this stuff!" I whispered back, holding my smoking cigarette vertical between our faces. "They asked me if I was smoking more but enjoying it less."

"Oh yeah, I remember that ad–they got you on that one, didn't they?" She chuckled.

"How could they miss? Anyone who is smoking at all is smoking more and enjoying it less! They got everybody!"

"And?"

"Well, I switched to their brand! Do you think for a minute that afterward I was smoking less and enjoying it more?"

"I don't know. Were you?"

"No! And that's exactly my point. These things don't satisfy at all!"

"You should have been suspicious when they put twenty of them in a pack Max"

"Funny! And the beer we drink; We drink one then we have another. they put six of them in a pack too you know! They don't satisfy either. You could say the same thing for pot, or acid, or any of that stuff."

"OK, I get it. Move on."

"I'm hungry for something Liz–looking for something," I caught myself getting louder again. "I feel like I have an emptiness inside, a void, a vacuum. It's like there's a hole in my soul!"

"I can identify with that. I guess I'm in the same boat. We probably all are."

Our conversation was cut short when a police cruiser came by. They drove slowly around the property, shining flashlights as they went as if they were looking for something. I suspect they had gotten a report of someone prowling around the station. The cruiser drove past the enclosure and shined the flash-light straight into my eyes. I didn't move a muscle. If they saw us they didn't act like it. They said nothing and just drove on.

After they were gone I said,

"Boy, am I glad they didn't see us. Do you have any idea how mad they would be if they caught us using a flag like this?" I had to get my gouge in. Liz simply said,

"That's why we covered up with it. So they wouldn't see us."

I had to admit that I was pretty convinced myself that they just thought someone had thrown a rag or something into the corner of the enclosure. That did it! Twice in one day she had been right and I had been wrong. I was through arguing with this girl. From now on, if she said it, I was going to do it. She was, after all, *The Prophetess*.

After a while, it got so cold that we decided to re-new our effort to find Al and Dave. The only lead we had left was the beach house, so we headed in what we thought was the direction of the Lake. We found a street called Lake Shore Drive so we figured we must be close. A number of cars were pulling boats behind them. Good sign, I thought. We knocked on the win-dows of several cars that were stopped at traffic lights asking them where the Lake was. We kept getting the same response. Most of the people wouldn't roll their windows down more than a crack. And they all asked the same thing; "What lake?" Even the ones pulling the boats didn't seem to have a clue what we were talk-ing about. I didn't get it. It seemed like a conspiracy. I thought it might have been because of the bad press we had gotten. Finally, exhausted, we threw ourselves down under a tree and tried to sleep; Liz on one side and me on the other. It was the coldest night I had ever spent. When the sun came up in the morning we discovered we had spent the night right on the beach! I could've thrown a rock and hit the water. No wonder we nearly froze! And no wonder people had responded with "What lake?" the night before. They no doubt all thought that we couldn't possibly mean something so obvious as Lake Erie.

We didn't find where Al and Dave were staying until that afternoon. They weren't there of course. They had gone to work at a berry farm early in the morning. When they got home, about six in the evening, imagine our surprise to see Rick with them. He had gotten the money for his fine the day before just as Liz and I had. But we were gone by the time he had been processed out. Somehow, by taking an alternative route he had beat us to Dave and Al's place. Everybody was smiles and hugs, and jumping up and down with elation. So we were together again —only minus the car. Man was it good to get a meal and sleep somewhere warm, even if it was on the floor.

The next morning, we all got up early. After a good breakfast of eggs and ham along with some eye electrifying coffee, we went to pick raspberries. Mostly Latinos worked at the berry farm. They came in families and were well equipped and trained for the job. You wouldn't think that berry picking would take much talent—until you try it. I remember watching those Latinos with their specially built trays strapped to the front of them loaded with quart baskets. They would literally *milk* the berries off the bushes into the baskets, filling them with great dexterity. I felt like I was trying to run a marathon against highly trained athletes. Even the littlest of their kids left me in the dust.

Generations of doing this must have helped these people make a quantum leap in the berry picking evolutionary process, I thought. But I wasn't alone. None of my friends could hold a candle to these mutated berry pluckers either. This was their time of the year to make money. Even though the owners paid us by the quart, the Latinos had to be making huge hourly wages.

It was quite different with my friends and I. Having not learned to "feel" for the berries, we had to actually *look* for them. For us, it was a one by one process. Filling one of those quart baskets was a monumental task. None of us were earning even close to minimum wage. We continued struggling through the process for several days, gaining little in ability or cash.

Eventually, we had a conference to decide where we were going from here. Al, Dave, and Rick still wanted to go to the World's Fair in Montreal. How to go was undecided since we had no vehicle. Liz said that it was time for us to go home and I agreed with her. She was, after all, *The Prophetess*, and I was not going to argue with her anymore. So it was decided that we would part ways.

The others graciously added to Liz and my meager funds so that we had enough to buy two bus tickets to Ohio. The next morning the others went back to the fruit farm for more berry-picking fun, while she and I made our way to the bus station. When we walked through the door the ticket clerk took one look at us and said,

"Let me guess–Toronto?"

The smart-aleck must have only half read the newspapers. He probably saw something about us headed for Canada and had it in his head that we were draft dodgers. Toronto was where most of them were going. Or maybe the papers mentioned something about Toronto in connection with us. To tell the truth I never did read any of the articles. We weren't allowed to read newspapers in jail, and vagrants don't have

31

enough money or time for them. They're too busy trying to not be vagrants. At least he didn't ask me about my religion. Anyway, we told him we wanted to go to Akron, Ohio but the closest our money would get us, was Cleveland. So we bought two tickets.

After settling into our seats, we began talking. Our conversation quickly turned to the subject of peace again.

"You know," I said "we hippies talk a good talk about peace; you know–the peace movement and all that, but the way I see it we don't get along any better than anyone else when it comes right down to it. We argue and fight just like the rest of the world–sometimes worse. And do you know why? It's because we're all dissatisfied!"

"I guess it's actually kinda hypocritical huh?" Liz noted. "If we don't have peace inside how could we possibly have peace with each other?"

"Yeah! It *has* to start on the inside!" I poked myself in the chest. "I guess that's it. I'm looking for peace!" I stopped for a moment then said in a voice of despair, "But I still don't know where to get it."

Liz suddenly became unusually serious, "Max, you're describing exactly how I feel."

"Well, I'm telling you one thing!" I declared, "*if I ever figure out where it's at–peace that is, I'll go to any extreme to get it!*"

And so, on our conversation ran as we traveled through Erie Pennsylvania, past Ashtabula, Ohio and on into Cleveland.

Upon disembarking our bus, we looked up the only place in town we knew. It was a coffeehouse called *The Well* on the East Side of town in the University Circle area of Case Western Reserve. I remember well our sitting in the small, dirty, dimly lit building at a little round table with Liz. We had enough money left to buy two coffees and a sandwich. I would have rather bought cigarettes but Liz said no, we were buying the sandwich. So I was still smoking cigarette butts I was picking up off the streets. While I was at the counter ordering the sandwich, I asked the man in charge where a person could find a place for the night.

"How many?" He inquired.

"Just the girl and me," I nodded at Liz.

"You guys can crash at my pad if you want. I usually got half a dozen or so anyway." He answered.

"Cool! Thanks man!"

"Hey! Don't mention it. What's a few more? Just wait around till closing time and you can go with me."

As Liz and I ate we listened to a bearded black man who sat in the corner on a platform reading some unrhyming poetry from a manuscript in a very monotone and mumbled voice. The poetry was done up to sound intellectual, but I thought it was actually just ambiguous. Maybe it was just me, but he seemed to be high on drugs, as did many of those sitting around listening. When he finished reading one piece the people weakly applauded. Then he started in on another. Liz seemed to be enjoying the whole thing but it was boring the socks off of me so I told her I was going to the head shop next door.

I felt more at home the moment I walked into the shop. *A Country Joe and the Fish* album was playing and lights were flashing around the room. The walls were lined with black light posters and hung with clothes you couldn't find anywhere else. The glass counters were filled with belt buckles, beads, pipes, hookahs, and Zigzag papers of every flavor. After hanging around a while I realized it was getting late and headed back to the coffeehouse.

Upon entering the building, I noticed that a threatening element had drifted in; a motorcycle gang. Some sported sleeveless denim jackets while others wore leather ones sporting the gang's colors. Their emblem was a colorful skull and crossbones with the large emblazoned word *PAGANS* arched over them; *PAGANS*. Now that really threw me a curve. Bible totin' bikers? What I knew about bikers put them light years away from what I knew a pagan to be. Could they actually be a different kind of bike gang? Maybe they had started reading the Bible too.

Then I noticed one of them sitting at the table with Liz being friendlier than I felt comfortable with. I was concerned that she might say tell him off. *Well, I'm sure two pagans can work out their differences*, I thought. So I carted my 6-foot, 135-pound body over to the table and said

"Hey!"

I noticed as the bearded man stood to his feet that he had the word President written across the front of his jacket. *Boy, can I pick 'em or what?*

"Yeah?" he responded.

Pagan or not, I was concerned about where this was going. But I had to do what I had to do to protect Liz. I summoned the meanest, most threatening voice I could muster.

"That's mine!" I declared firmly pointing at her.

He simply looked at me for a moment then said in an apologetic voice,

"Well, I'm sorry man. I didn't know,"

"Oh, that's OK. No harm done," I said, nearly fainting.

"Here, let me buy you guys a coke or something," he insisted.

With that, he walked over to the counter.

As soon as his back was turned I whispered to Liz through clenched teeth.

"Let's get out of here as soon as we can!"

"Good idea! I'm with you on this one," She said out of the corner of her mouth.

34

A moment later the President came back with three drinks and sat them on the table.

"Mind if I join you for a second?" he asked.

What was I going to say? *Get lost?* Not hardly.

"Sure, pull up a chair," I invited.

Our conversation was mostly small talk at first; exchanging of names and so forth. I told him that we were from Akron and shared our Dunkirk story with him. He knew all about Dunkirk. He had been stopped there himself. It was a speed trap. As our conversation loosened up a little I couldn't help but ask why they chose the name *Pagans* for their gang.

"Because that pretty much says it all, man. That's what we are!" he puffed out his chest.

"So are we!" I responded excitedly, noticing that same puzzled look registering on Liz's face.

"Well, I sure know that you've got guts. And I respect that," He looked at me.

"Do you guys believe the devil's real?" I asked him. Little did he know that I was running a test on him.

"Seen him myself." he answered coldly.

"And do you believe that God answers prayer?" I continued to the second stage of the test. Now I noticed a puzzled look on his face.

"I don't believe in God!" He swore firmly. "Like I said, I'm a pagan!"

"Yeah I know you are. But how can you be a pagan and not believe in God?" I asked.

The president slammed his closed fist on the table, which rocked a bit causing our drinks to dance.

"What do you mean?" he demanded, "that's what a pagan is!"

I must've touched on a sore spot.

"Oh!" was all I said. *Far be it from me to disagree.* I quickly changed the subject and our conversation returned to a measure of normalcy. And for your

35

information, the president did not pass the test. In a few minutes, he said

"Well, it's been real nice chattin' with you folks but we gotta get on down the road."

With that, he rose to his feet, put both little fingers into the corners of his mouth and let out the most ear-splitting whistle I had ever heard. Everybody stopped what they were doing and looked his way.

"Let's Ride!!" he bellowed making a follow me motion with his hand as if he were leading his cavalry into a charge. They all enthusiastically responded with shouts of

"Yeah!" As if they just lived to be on the road with their Harley's. After the horde of twentieth-century pirates Pagans swarmed out of the place, saddled up and roared down Euclid Avenue I said to Liz.

"We need to ride too. Let's clear out."

Once outside Liz said, "We can't stay with that man behind the bar. It's not safe. In fact, we need to get out of here *now*!" That was fine by me. I was more than ready to 'get out of there' even though it was dark and we had no place to go. Just then I looked up the street and saw about twenty white helmets bobbing down the sidewalk in our direction. It was a police riot squad.

"It's some kind of a raid!" I yelled at Liz. "Come on, let's get outta here!"

We had no reason to run except that we didn't need to get caught in the middle of anything else. So we took off just as the police were pouring into the head shop and coffeehouse.

That evening we learned the nightspots of Cleveland—sleeping spots that is. We started the night beside the lagoon in front of the Art Museum.

As we lay beside the lagoon starring deeply into the starry sky, I said,

"Now there, in *the Well* tonight, with the bikers, we have a perfect example of what you and I were talking about earlier. I don't care if they are pagans they have no peace inside. They're discontented. They question their own self-worth and have to try to prove that they're somebody by terrorizing everyone else.

"Well Max," Liz said, "you put on a pretty tough act yourself, standing up to that president."

"Yeah—but that was a matter of self-preservation!" I argued.

"Maybe theirs' is too," she suggested.

"Well, it's a perfect illustration of what I said before. We can't have peace with each other because we don't have peace within. The whole world is full of trouble because of it.

"Yeah, I see your point," she agreed. Then pointing to the sky she asked, "Look, aren't they just beautiful?"

Then suddenly she turned, looked full in my face and with the most serious expression imaginable said,

"Max, when you find it, I want you to come back and tell me where it is."

"Find what Liz?" I asked, looking deep into her eyes.

"Peace," was all she said as she returned her gaze to the stars.

"Of course I will," I answered, "you know I would. And I hope you'd do the same for me."

"Of course I will," She said.

As we lay on the ground looking up at the stars Liz casually asked, "By the way. Max, what do you think the word *pagan* means?"

"Well, Rick said it's someone who has their own interpretation of the Bible," I looked at her.

Liz began to laugh.

"What's so funny?" I asked.

37

"That's not what pagan means! A pagan is some-body who isn't a Christian, Jew or Muslim. It means a heathen!" she said between gasps for breath.

"What?!" I responded in shock. "No! Tell me that's not so!" This was a real epiphany.

"You know Rick isn't any good at English," Liz re-minded me by now snorting in her laughter.

Half embarrassed and certainly disappointed, I said, "Oh, I know. But man! I was so excited to have a word that described us,"

"I'm sorry," she managed to get out. "But this is so funny!"

It was really cold that night–again. There were so many people coming and going past the lagoon that we decided to head somewhere else. So we moved to a fire escape in an alley, but after being scared by someone coming down the alley we moved to the sidewalk in front of a bar because it was well lit. Besides, we felt safer with people around. Then we got nervous about the *kind* of people that were around, so we finished the night in the Greyhound bus station. When they de-manded that we get out I was so dead asleep that Liz couldn't rouse me. She said I started swinging my arms and legs wildly every time she tried. She would poke me then jump back. Once I calmed down she would do it again. I finally woke up but by then it was morning.

We eventually got a ride to Akron later that day. We went to my parent's house. I don't think I ever saw anyone so glad to get a shower as Liz was. After that, she went home. I was elated to sleep in my own bed again.

In the end, none of us ever got to Expo 67 (the World's Fair in Montreal.) Everybody ended up back in Akron, within a few weeks.

Rick never did make the trip to Dunkirk to retrieve his impounded Buick. So, the County of Chautauqua in New York got a free car. I had found out that we weren't pagans, so it was back to Istinity. I had so hoped that I had found a proper name for us. I was sick of having to explain Istinity all the time. At least we weren't vagrants anymore. But then this was 1967 and the summer of love was still young.

But now for the question: How do two people such as Liz and myself, on so sincere a quest, get so far from what they are looking for? During our excursion to Dunkirk and back we both defined precisely what we were after, yet neither of us had a clue where to find it, or if it existed at all. Neither did any of our friends. Our search for significance and satisfaction had only led us to places where they could not be found and to things that could never give them. They had all turned out to be dead end streets. We were lost and so far from our destiny. *How did we get here*?

I can't altogether answer for Liz. I knew little about the woman beyond her beauty. As for myself; how did I get here? Well as Shakespeare has it–"*thereby hangs my tale.*"

CHAPTER 2

WRITER'S CRAMP

The ground was covered with a blanket of undisturbed snow as the sun came peeping over the eastern horizon. Tree branches were laden thick with the white stuff, which sparkled in the rising sun. The crisp cold air had not the slightest breeze stirring. Big, thick, flakes had filled the air the evening before, falling so fast that to stand still was to have them pile up on you. It had been the perfect Christmas Eve with the colored lights shining beautifully through the descending snow.

It was difficult getting to sleep that night but in its own time slumber overtook me and carried me off to wherever it is you go when you lose consciousness. Next thing I knew the morning came with the sun beating down on my bedroom window, forcing its way through the curtains' cracks. The sweet songs of the birds drew me slowly up out of the deep well of sleep. I gradually became conscious of their carols, which were so merry that for some time I lay listening. Then I noticed; aside from the birds, it was uncommonly quiet. Suddenly it hit me,

"This is Christmas morning!"

I scrambled out from under the covers and scurried across their top to the window. Pulling back the curtain told the tale. Sure enough–overnight, while we slept, our neighborhood had been transformed into a wonderland where you might expect to see elves peeking out from behind rocks and trees.

Later that morning we opened presents. I got most of the things I had wished for, but for me the main event of the morning came as I was tearing the paper away from one of the gifts and the writing on the box beneath came into view piece by piece. *YES! This was it! The very thing I had asked for and dreamed of; a portable Royal typewriter!*

Now it may seem like a strange thing that a twelve-year-old would ask for a typewriter as his main Christmas present–but we all ask in accordance with our dreams, and I had dreamed about words all my life. I had been fascinated with them. I loved the study of the words themselves; where they came from, what they meant, and how they worked as well as the way people strung them together. Even their sounds in some strange way had a therapeutic effect upon me. But it was not enough to experience the way others assembled them. I wanted to marshal the hosts of expression myself. I had no idea of success at it. The process itself and the creating of a finished product were what I loved. I may have been suffering from delusions of grandeur but I thought that I could paint pictures with words. At any rate, it gave me great personal satisfaction and an inward sense of well-being to try. It was as if giving expression to my inner self on paper scratched some itch way down inside. I instinctively knew that for me–to write was to be.

I loved reading almost as much as writing. I was especially taken with the classics and read them vivaciously. Above all I loved poetry. I would be held in awe as I read those beautiful expressions of the soul. I could hardly believe that human ingenuity was capable of such cunning. Often, I memorized long passages of it, particularly Shakespeare.

But don't for a moment misinterpret the gift of the typewriter as my parents' approval of these tendencies. They liked them no better, and for that matter understood them no more, than they did my love for Mozart and Beethoven. These were country and western folks with some pop music thrown in here and there: Hank Williams or maybe even Elvis–but classical music? Give them a break! They just wanted their son to be normal. For crying out loud the kid wouldn't even live up to his nickname *Butch* by being a scraper! The typewriter was nothing more than a compromise in the ongoing struggle between their values and their only kid's independence. Their whole system was being challenged by the nitty-gritty reality of raising this child. They had a different pattern in mind for him than the way he was turning out. I think they wondered where they had gone wrong. Nobody else in the family had ever acted maladjusted like this.

The reason, other than the affordable price, I had requested a portable typewriter, in particular, was so I could take it with me wherever I went. Then I would always be ready to write at a moment's notice, which would be especially helpful when I was with my best friend, Terry Thrash. He was afflicted with the same literary disorder as myself. Almost daily we got together to feed our malady by sharing our compositions with one another for critique, suggestions, and inspiration. We also loved the works of other wordsmiths and would share passages from their writings and discuss them. These gatherings formed a sort of unofficial writer's club which eventually grew to four: Terry Thrash, Roger Paul Lester Lowe and me.

As with most authors, our writings came chiefly from our own personal experiences. Like most boys our age, we craved adventure. In fact, it was the single common thread running through the works of all our favorite writers. We reveled in their swashbuckling tales of pirates and knights, espionage and intrigue. I dreamed that one day I would be a soldier of fortune myself, hunting down lost treasures and hiring myself out for mercenary causes. That would surely give me something to write home about.

To have stories to tell we actually sought out adventure. Looking back, I now realize that it was just another avenue of searching in my pursuit for inner peace. Anything for a thrill to spice up the internal boredom I endured daily.

We were not quite as extreme as the legendary Kit Carson, whose writers, we are told, sometimes published his experiences before they actually happened, after which he would live them out so they would be true. At least we waited until after our exploits to tell the tale. But we were undeniably on a quest for the Holy Grail of writing material, or so we thought. We didn't have to look far to find what we were after–look for trouble and it will find you.

But it was Lester through whom I was introduced to another side of life. I first connected with him through his younger brother, Junior, who I met at school. Junior was a year or so younger than I, so we didn't spend much time together, but he came to me one day with a message from his older brother, Lester, who had been wheelchair bound for the biggest part of a year but wanted to meet me.

The story of Lester and my meeting includes the tale of a couple of buildings in our part of town. Across the road from where Parkwood Avenue, the street I lived on, ended at Union Street, stood the locally owned Jewish grocery store, behind which an enormous 10 story, 60–apartment tenement building filled the horizon as it loomed against the sky. The dirty red brick structure, which predated the civil war, looked down on our neighborhood like an ancient centennial. It had the very aura of evil about it. Only the bottom five or six floors were used as apartments. None of us knew what took place on the top floors. Nothing in any of the apartments we broke into. Still, we suspected prostitution was happening in some of the ones we couldn't get into. We weren't sure we knew where all the apartments were anyway. There were rumors of a shooting gallery for heroin addicts somewhere up there. It was said that dealing drugs was what put the building's owner in the penitentiary. I knew for sure there was bootlegging going on in at least one of the apartments.

It was a great place for exploration not only because of the empty apartments but there was also the basement and the attic. The cellar was a cross between a web–filled cavern, a crypt, and a dark, dank dungeon with a labyrinth that connected the many dirt–floored rooms where the rats lived. An occasional shaft of light cutting through the dark where there was crack enough between the boards over the windows to permit it was the only source of seeing.

The huge, open, football field sized attic, which was broken up only by brick support columns, had a more diffused light that filled the entire area with a ghostly gray-green cast. It was too dim to see from one end to the other. But what little the light did reveal was eerie. Everything was covered with the dust and cobwebs of many years. Scattered throughout the attic were pieces of abandoned furniture, mostly dressers and tables, from long ago. Two rickety wooden sets of stairs, one at either end of the huge room, led to unlocked doors that opened out onto the large flat roof. Bats hung in abundance from the ceiling beams above.

Bats and rats were seldom seen in the apartments, but the roaches more than made up for them, and I don't mean a few. Open a pantry door at night and inside it would be completely covered with them; thousands of the grotesque creatures would scramble over

top one another to escape the light, creating a sicken-
ing rustling paper sound which haunts me to this day.

The place was also perfect breeding grounds for future gangsters. The bigger part of its' inhabitants had
come out of the mountains of the south, mostly West
Virginia, looking for the better life that a job in the big
city could provide. I'm not sure why the better life
never happened for most of those people. I do know
that vice of all type, and drink, in particular, plagued
the place and violence was a way of life. Another thing
I came to know is that if you want to create some ex-
traordinarily malicious street gangs, take a group of
boys out of the wooded hills of Appalachia and turn
them loose in the inner city; the rest will take care of
itself.

Among the families living in the bowels of this be-
hemoth building was the Lowes. Seven children; three
boys and four girls, along with their parents made up
the clan. The population of their apartment would
usually be half again that number at any given time.
The whole family had a "there's always room for one
more" attitude that made it an easy place for the children's friends to congregate. And if the kids liked you
the parents pretty much adopted you. This was the
place I had to go to in order to meet Lester.

I became a special case with Lester's family. More
than others, I became part of the woof and warp of the
Lowe family. While they proved to be my ticket to the
adventure I was seeking, I knew not that I had stepped
into the mouth of a dragon that would eventually de-
vour me.

When Lester and I first met, I discovered that his
interest lay in what he had heard about my writing. He
had a project he wanted someone to work with him on,
which is where the story of the second building comes
in.

"I've been researching the history of Hower House," he said, referring to the three and a half story, 28 room Victorian mansion on Fir Hill.

"How's it coming?" I asked to be congenial.

"Fair, but I need more specific information: you might say *inside* information."

"Inside information?" I repeated, mostly to myself.

"Yes, I can look up the history and stuff like that, but there's nothing about what the inside is like."

"How do you plan to get in?"

"That's just it. I can't. It will still be a while before I can get out of this wheelchair. I need someone to do the footwork for me."

"Well I'm actually trying to get more into writing adventure stories," I said glancing at a copy of Haggard's *King Solomon's Mines* lying on the table beside Lester's bed.

"I can relate," he said, "but let me tell you if it's action you want to write about, just hang around here a while and you'll find it."

"Really?" I said, "Well, maybe I'll find something to write about while I'm working with you."

"Then it's a deal?" Lester asked.

"Sure. But let me ask; —why the Hower House?"

"Personal interest I guess. There's just something about the place that fascinates me."

"Any ideas on where to start?"

"Not a clue. I hear that the lady who lives there is kind of funny about letting people see inside the place. She even has the first-floor windows covered with inside shutters," he said.

"And I've heard that her name is Mrs. Crawford," I added, "They say that she owns diamond mines in Africa or somewhere. Don't worry, I'll think of something to get on the inside," I assured Lester.

True to my word Roger Paul and I did get inside the Hower House. We did it by posing as reporters from Central High School's student newspaper. The school stood just across the street from the backside of the mansion, but neither Roger nor I had ever so much as set foot inside the place, its lowest grade being the ninth and we having attained only unto the eighth. Whether the lady of the house, who was called by the maid that answered the door, actually bought our story or was just humoring a couple of curious kids to help pass a boring afternoon, I will never know. But the two of us were given a most magnificent personal tour of the main floor of the mansion by Grace Crawford, who had lived there since 1918. A museum would have had nothing over on this place. The walls and pillars were hung thick with shields, swords, spears, halberds, muskets, helmets, tapestries and flags. The central room even had human skulls from New Guinea atop each of four main doors into it. There was an actual treasure chest and an authentic suit of armor. It was, hands down, one of the most thrilling experiences of my youth. I took copious notes and returned to Lester who sat and wrote his own as I read from mine, stopping me every few lines to ask questions for further information or clarity.

Relaying the results of my research to Lester cemented our friendship, which lasted for years. His family turned out to be my entry point into the dark system of shadows that cast themselves over every part of our city, for his family was friends with everyone in the building, and the building's roots wormed their way through the squalid underground of the entire metropolitan area.

As to Lester's promise of adventure looking me up, it certainly did. It arrived packaged as street gangs, booze, drugs, crime and vice of every description; this was to become *my dragon*.

Eventually, I came to be a member of two rival street gangs at the same time. I had each convinced that I was only in the other as a spy. Then I would divulge just enough information–part of it fabricated – to keep my charade going. I soon discovered a great sense of power when I realized that I could control entire groups of people and events by the information flow I provided. While I knew that it was a dangerous game in which I was engaged, I failed to appreciate exactly how precarious the position I had placed myself in was. Therefore, it was a risk that I was willing to run; this playing both ends against the middle, not only for the adventure of it, but to boost my sagging self–esteem.

Then one of our gang members, –*Peanuts*, in a drunken rage, nearly beat a mailman to death with a monkey wrench. When pressed for a reason he simply said,

"I didn't like the way he looked at me."

Until then I thought that most of these boys, being from the hills of Appalachia had no idea what inner city street gangs were supposed to be like. I thought that I, having been raised in Chicago, had the corner on that information. It was my mistaken notion that most of them were simply playing a more advanced variation of cops and robbers. I had yet to learn how rapidly humans can adapt to their surroundings. Only after Peanuts arrest and subsequent incarceration did it dawn upon me why many of these guys carried weapons. It was then that I realized the possible calamity course I had put myself on. What had I been thinking?

Realizing my perilous predicament, I began carrying weapons for protection myself. I got hold of a blackjack, then a 16–inch gravity knife, and eventually a blank gun that I thought might at least scare off any would-be attackers. I made it a point to advertise the fact that I was always armed. I began my own publicity campaign to create a specific public image, depicting myself as a half–crazed animal mutilator who had no honor and was not above stabbing someone in the back. I touted myself as having a vengeful streak that was beyond my control and that I was likely to mete out retribution against any offender, regardless of gang affiliation by jumping them at night in a dark alley when they least expected it. My Dad always told me that the most dangerous man was the scared one who had been backed into a corner.

"A man like that is likely to do anything," He would say.

I was that man, well–at least I was that boy.

And of course, there were the other gangs to be concerned about as well. One of the most notorious of them was on our side of town. They named themselves after the main drag that ran through the middle of their turf calling themselves *the Upson Street Gang*. They imposed a 9:00 pm curfew on their entire neighborhood, including the adults, which they enforced by patrolling the streets with an old step van, carrying baseball bats, tire irons, choker chains, knives and occasional guns.

Jim Cook, ever wirey and cold as steel, a clear product of his environment, was the head of the Upson Street Gang. He was your typical hood. Jim might have been an entrepreneur in any other environment, but here he was simply top dog.

There came a day when Jim, with some of his gang, caught me walking through their neighborhood and stopped me.

"Where do you think you're going?" Jim acted as spokesman for the group that surrounded me.

"Look, I'm just passing through, I don't want any trouble. I'm just on my way home," I said.

"Well, it looks like trouble has found you!" Jim retorted.

"Com'on guys. Look, I won't come through here anymore—ok?" I pleaded.

"Oh, don't worry about that!" Jim said, "I know you won't when I'm done with you."

"Hey man, I'm serious! I'll stay out of your turf," I still affirmed.

"Come on, I want you to fight me," He said putting up his fists as he started to dance around.

"I'm not going to fight you," I replied.

"Oh yes you are. You don't have any choice," He declared as he continued to dance.

"Do what you have to do, I'm not going to fight you," I said.

"Then I want to see you shake," He demanded.

Even though I was terrified, I was too proud to let him humiliate me. So I extended my hand and said,

"OK. Put'er there partner."

Jim was absolutely shocked,

"You smart aleck! I said I want to see you shake!" He shouted in my face, slapping my hand away.

"And I said put'er there," I repeated sticking my hand out again. Some of the other gang members chuckled.

"Boy, are you gonna get it!" He said in a rage.

I turned and started to walk away but he came after me. Grabbing me by the collar he spun me around to face him with his fist drawn back. I didn't flinch, and the blow never came. Jim just stood and stared at me in disbelief. He slowly lowered his fist.

"I'm not going to fight you, Jim," I categorically said, using his name.

"You know me?" he asked.

"Yeah, everybody knows about Jim Cook. You've got a reputation you know," I answered.

"Really now! What kind of a reputation? And you'd better make this good," He said.

"I didn't make the reputation Jim. I just heard it," I responded.

"And what did you hear?"

"That you're tough. Nobody wants to mess with you."

"Go on."

"And your gang is a legend!"

"You heard about me, so you won't fight me. That was good sense on your part. But you didn't cower down either. You got guts and sense. Now there's a rare combination. What's your name?"

"Max," I said "Max Wood."

One of the other gang members spoke up,

"Not the Max Wood that knows Lester Lowe?" he asked.

"Yeah, that's me. Lester and I are best friends," I declared. To evidence the fact I added, "And I know his brothers Robert and Junior and his sisters too."

The same boy said,

"I'm Dave Holiday–his cousin," as he stepped forward and extended his hand. "He talks about you all the time."

"Great!" I said with a level of relief that was detectable.

"Hey, I hear from Lester that you carry a monster switchblade," Dave said.

"Well, it's not a switchblade. It's actually a gravity knife," I explained using the word for a non–spring operated knife that could be locked open instantly with a flick of the wrist.

"Well let's see it," Jim said.

"Sure," I pulled the 16–inch knife out of my pocket. Dave took it and looked it over.

"Let me see it," Jim took it from him and turned it over a few times, inspecting it, then handed it back to me.

"How does it work?" he asked. "Show me."

I flicked my wrist and for the first time since I owned the thing, it didn't open. Stage fright I'm sure. I was intimidated. I tried again only harder. This time, it opened halfway just before flying out of my hand. Everybody shrieked, ducking as the knife went sailing through the crowd and hit the biggest boy present in the chest with a *thunck*. He screamed thinking he'd been stabbed. The knife landed on the ground in its half–opened position. Shaking, the boy picked it up and holding it in both hands gingerly offered it back to me as if it were a religious sacrifice.

"That's quite a weapon if you can figure out how to use it," Jim joked, looking around at his boys who joined him in laughter.

"Actually, that's the first time I've had a problem with it," I replied, and then demonstrated several times with no mishaps.

Jim spoke,

"I'll tell you what. If you're a friend of Dave's, Max, you're a friend of mine. You're ok by me. You can pass through here anytime. And if anyone gives you any trouble you just tell them Jim Cook said for them to leave you alone."

"Thanks, man. I appreciate it," I said relieved.

"Tell Lester I said hi," Dave mentioned.

"Sure thing," I answered glad to be walking away with my life. And walk away is exactly what I did.

From that time on Jim and I were friendly acquaintances. I had no desire to be close enough a friend to become part of his world. But it gave me more writing material. On a cold winter's afternoon not long after our meeting, Jim and I skipped school together and hung out in the basement of his house. He was drinking hard liquor, which opened him up just enough to start talking about his dreams and aspirations for life.

He was thinking about selling a motor scooter he had and using the money to buy a junk car and head for Mexico. He wanted to see Tijuana where he had heard you could buy all the marijuana a person could want. He asked if I would like to go along. I was flattered that he would ask me over any of his gang members, but I knew I couldn't. I had a family, a mother, and father that would never let it happen. The law would be on my tail quicker than I could get out of the state. But I didn't tell Jim that. He wouldn't have understood anyway. No one ever cared enough about him to trouble themselves with where he went or what he did. I just made up an excuse. The following year Jim did disappear for most of the summer vacation. When he came back he was driving a red convertible with a white top, telling stories of Mexarkana, and was dark enough to be a Mexican himself.

About a week after our afternoon in Jim's basement someone at school made a derogatory remark about Max Wood, and Jim Cook gave them the beating of their life. So I came to be accepted by the most violent gang on our side of town.

Since crime is a way of life with gangs it's not surprising that I became a thief, breaking into cars, houses, and businesses. Since I held nothing sacred churches, because they were such easy prey, became one of my preferred targets. I tried to learn how to pick pockets and did become a practiced shoplifter. I would have an item off the shelf, hid on my person and be out the door quicker than proprietors knew what had hit them. I thought I was pretty clever—until I got caught that is. I now know that all thieves are eventually caught, it is just a matter of time. I eventually began to be reeled into a network of organized crime resulting in numerous altercations with the law.

Somewhere in the middle of all this, life began to take an unpleasant turn for me. The sexual perversions with which I was confronted especially shocked my naive mind. Seeing the ugly underside of the prostitution empire left me stunned enough, but when I personally stumbled upon the naked, twisted, decomposing corpse of one of the ladies of the night, indignation against the injustice of their system was set to seething within me. It was also the first time I had a chance to witness the laxity of the legal system when it came to such cases, which further enraged my sense of justice.

And it was bad enough to deal with the all-too-common propositions made to us younger men by our older counterparts in those squalid slums but when I witnessed firsthand the molestation of a friend by one of them I was left traumatized.

I may have begun with romantic notions about adventure, but the exploitations that I came to witness did not square at all with what I had anticipated.

It was an ugly world where the big fish ate the little fish, and I was a little fish. Everyone lived by his or her own law and there was little mercy. I had gotten in too deep. I was getting burned. *My adventure was mutating into the dragon.*

One of the gangs I was part of operated in the Howard Street area, which was Akron's skid row district where they averaged a murder a night. I began going among the very people who were doing the murdering and being murdered. They were the gutter alcoholics and homeless drug addicts whose lives had been reduced to nothing more than animal status. I would go to the very places the murders were being committed:

along the canal, under the bridges, and in the abandoned buildings. But I wasn't there for a visit: I was on a mission. I first bought my way into the vagabond's favor with cans of food and bags of beans taken from our family's cupboard, but later I would give one of them enough money to buy two pints of wine. Usually they got the biggest bang for their buck by making the purchase in the back room of an empty storefront where they bootlegged the poison. One of the two pints I sent them to buy was for themselves; that was the bribe, the other was for me. I would find a place to be alone and in an attempt to escape the oppressing world my life had become; *my dragon*, I would drink to sink myself in an ocean of oblivion. Perhaps more than escaping I was trying to fill the growing emptiness I had begun to feel within. It was but a poor substitute for the peace that I was pursuing.

In time, I found opportunity to turn to drugs. During my first experience, I entered into a world of fantasy that was as real to me as this one. It was more than a new thrill or a better kick for me; it was a much more effective escape. Drugs, for me, proved to be the quickest road out of my situation and an even more effective way of silencing the now screaming hunger pangs I felt inside. This too had its cost. There was a price to be paid, and I found myself paying it, you might say, with a pound of flesh. *The dragon was taking his toll.*

Then several of my friends were killed. Two of them were Lester's brothers. One was electrocuted by twice the voltage of an electric chair. The other brother, Junior, was ambushed by a rival gang and shot-gunned to death.

Two more of my friends, Fuzzy McGraw and Jerry Derringer, had been drinking and went into the most dangerous bar in the Howard Street area demanding to be served. When the bartender refused, Fuzzy grabbed a bottle, broke it over the counter, and threatened him with it. With that, the bartender pulled a gun from behind the counter, chased them out of the establishment, down the street and trapped them in a doorway where he shot them both to death. Fuzzy and Jerry were only fifteen. Skid row murder is no respecter of age.

Another of my friends, Joe Little, was gunned down during a grocery store robbery. Then there was the lady whose home was one of our main hangouts who was beaten to death by her drunken husband. It was such a brutal slaying that the walls were covered with blood. Some of our gang members helped clean up the mess in her memory.

Yes, I found much to write about. More, in fact, than I had bargained for. But the writing had fallen to the side. I found myself lost and getting into seriously troubled waters; it was a very dark place;

> *The dragon drew apace,*
> *Now coming on post haste.*

My world-view, which had once been filled with glamorous ideals, became increasingly more pessimistic as I grew into a cynic before my time. There was no humoring myself; I saw nothing to smile about, nothing to laugh at. My entire world had turned into despair, which only served to augment the yearning I felt within for some greater meaning to life. Hope began to flicker and then died within me. The dragon had me in its grip and had begun feeding on my rotting soul; consuming it, piece by putrid piece. There appeared to be no escaping now.

Then with an impeccable timing that suggested something more than was immediately obvious, the educational system told me that I was nothing more than a higher form of biological being. Part of the packaging that came with that explanation for our existence is the *survival of the fittest* philosophy. That just made sense if what they said was true.

But then the same teachers tried to tell us that certain behaviors were acceptable while others were not. Now where did that come from? Who's to tell anyone what's right or wrong if all we are is high-class animals? And where did they get the authority to do so? I got the notion that life was not meant to be fought with *Marquis de Queensbury* rules; the only thing that mattered was winning–*the survival of the fittest!*

That was the point at which the rage within me began to grow and replace the craving I had once felt. At first, I thought I was angry with God, but then I realized that there was nothing suggesting that there was a God. There did not seem to be any intelligent design to life. Everything I had witnessed appeared to be random at best and chaotic at worse. There was nothing personal in all of this–just cold dead chance. There couldn't be a God.

I felt ripped off and angry that I had been forced to arrive at such a conclusion. *Somebody should have to pay for this! I didn't even ask to be in this world,* I reflected. If this was all there was to it then I wasn't sure life was worth the bother. There should be something more–even if there wasn't.

And so it was that the intense dissatisfaction I had previously felt turned into hatred and got down into the functional level of my psyche. The rage within me caused what had once been my silent crime spree to erupt into confrontation as I began bullying those I dared, extorting anyone weaker than myself, and intimidating even the stronger using any equalizer I could lay hold of. It was my personal reign of terror and it was terror itself that became my weapon of choice. For my friends crime was more about money but to me, that was just a bonus; it was power and vengeance that I was after; the power to intimidate, which give me a sense of control in an out of control life. I suspect that my profile was probably beginning to resemble the *modus operandi* of a serial killer. I was indeed capable of murder and contemplated both it and self-destruction at times. *The dragon had devoured me; I was now, in fact, a little dragon myself.*

CHAPTER 3

TESTIMONY!

I grew to hate life. I felt as hollow inside as an empty fifty–five-gallon drum. This was doing my soul–if I had one–no good. I was an angry young man!

I distinctly recall, at that point of my life, riding in the backseat of my uncle's car one afternoon, when a billboard advertising whiskey slipped by. "*Smooth as silk,*" it said. I knew better. A horrible sense of insecurity came over me. I'm not precisely sure why the billboard had that effect on me; perhaps I was being better acquainted with the liquid devil inside that bottle than I wanted to be, for I did know him up closer and more personal than I was comfortable with, or maybe I saw in that bottle something that was bringing misery and heartbreak into my life.

Whatever the reason, it was at that precise moment that I thought I had an impression within me that was akin to hearing a voice with some other kind of faculty than we generally use; a voice that seemed to command conviction. I thought as I watched the billboard slide away that this voice pressed upon me,

"*Son there is a deeper meaning to life than you can see on the surface. There is an eternal purpose for mankind as a whole and for you as an individual.*"

A faint glimmer of hope flickered within me that if there was anything to this inner voice, I might have a destiny of some sort. Maybe there was a deeper meaning to life than could be seen on the surface. Perhaps the religions of the world were onto something about there being another side to things; a spirit world of some sort. They all shared an almost universal agreement on the idea. I found my own instincts wanting to agree with them. I felt that there ought to be a bigger scheme of things. Though in denial, I believe I was envious of those who had faith. But how could I be intellectually honest and give credence to what flew in the face of fact?

On the other hand, if the objective world around me was all there was then why didn't coming to terms with the fact give me the inner satisfaction that should accompany the discovery of truth.

The back-seat incident reflects a pattern that emerged in my life. I vacillated back and forth, wrestling with myself over how to interpret life, and what to do with mine. I wanted to have faith even if I was not able to justify it. These were heavy ponderings for someone my age, but they were my ponderings nonetheless.

That was when Ronnie Garlow first entered my life. Ronnie, who belonged to one of the street gangs in our part of town was one of the most feared boys on the East Side. But something happened. Ronnie quit the gang. And that wasn't all. He quit smoking, drinking, and drugs. It didn't take me long to find out why. Approaching me one day, he said,

"I want to show you something," as he rolled up his sleeve revealing an ugly four–inch scar that ran diagonally across the underside of his forearm.

"Wow!" I said looking at it.

"Do you know how I got that?" he asked.

"No," I looked from the scar to his face.

Ronnie began relating his story to me.

"During a gang fight in an alley one night I got knocked out. Probably hit with a blackjack or something. When I came back to my senses everyone was gone. I tried to get up but couldn't; too weak. Then I noticed my arm was slashed–really bad. Blood was pouring out."

"What did you do?"

"I tried to get up but slipped in my own blood and fell back down on the bricks. Then I prayed. I said, "God if You will spare me I will serve you." And you know what?"

"No. What?"

"In just a few minutes somebody came through that alley and nearly stumbled over my body. They called an ambulance and I was rushed to the hospital. That's how I got this scar," he stuck his arm out further.

"So you're saying God sent those people through the alley?"

"What do you think?"

"I dunno."

"Of course God sent them through the alley," he sarcastically retorted.

Ronnie was ever after convinced–there was no talking him out of it, nothing would do but that God had answered his prayer. He continued,

"And I was true to my word too. I went to church and began to serve the Lord! A lot of people make promises to God in a hot spot. There aren't any atheists in foxholes you know. But most of them never follow through with their promises. When the trouble's over they forget all about God, but the Bible says that we need to keep the promises we make to Him."

Ronnie had been telling his story to everybody around. He called it his *testimony*, and he delighted in repeating it. *Testimony*? What did he mean by that? What was he testifying to? Just sounded like a story to me. Maybe his story was supposed to prove something . . . he usually ended up making some kind of point like,

"God can change your life too if you let Him."

Whether I agreed with Ronnie or not I had to admit that he was certainly consistent about his religion. It was all he would talk about. We nicknamed him *The Preacher Boy*. He began handing out religious books among some of my friends. I remember Lester read one called *Raptured!* and showed me a chart that he had gotten from somewhere about the plan of the ages. It looked like blueprints for a house to me. The chart ended with those who were ready when the end came getting to spend eternity in heaven. The rest ended up in a lake of fire that was illustrated at the far end of the chart. Lester seemed to be earnestly interested. I thought it was probably nothing more than a fascination with the talent displayed in the drawing of the diagram. After all, Lester was a good draftsman. While I had to concede that the message of the book and the chart definitely spoke to Lester it was all lost on me; entirely over my head.

The Preacher Boy gave me no books. No, for me he reserved a much less cerebral and more direct approach. It started the day he sauntered up to me,

"Do you love Jesus?" he asked pointing at me with his index finger. I didn't want him to find out that I didn't know for sure who Jesus was so I told him the only thing I could think of:

"Well sure I do!" as if to say, *Doesn't everybody?*

"Well if you love him you'll be a *testimony* for him," Ronnie informed me. There was that word again.

"What's that?" I asked.

"Like I just *testified* to you," he said.

"Oh, well that's no big deal," I said, still not understanding and hoping he would just go away.

"Well, do you see those kids over there across the street?" he asked pointing to a group of street urchins standing against a wall.

"Yeah," I replied dubiously.

"If you love Jesus why don't you go over there and testify to them," he challenged me.

I was in shock, I was being told to do something I didn't even understand. But because of my own deceit, I was already in over my head so there was nothing to do but wade on through to the other side. I turned and headed toward the children thinking to myself as I stepped off the curb into the street,

Here goes everything.

I walked up to the children and pointed my index finger at them as if it were a gun, just like The Preacher Boy had done to me.

"Do you love Jesus?" I demanded in the most authoritative tone I could conjure up. It probably sounded like I was going to give them a thumping they would never forget if they didn't come up with the right answer. The blank look that came over their faces in all probability resembled the one that had come over mine when The Preacher Boy had asked me the same question. But, like myself, they didn't want their interrogator to think that they were ignorant and didn't know who Jesus was so they told me the only thing they could think of,

"Sure, I love Jesus!" said the biggest, "Don't you Jake?" He asked looking at the one next to him.

Jake shook his head,

"Sure, I love Jesus," he parroted. Then looking at the little girl beside him asked her,

"Don't you Sally?"

Sally shook her head affirmatively as well.

"Sure! I love Jesus!" she said looking at both Jake and the older boy.

"Yep! We all love Jesus," the eldest reiterated. With my mission completed, I went back across the street and gave my report to The Preacher Boy. . .

"Yep! They love Jesus—just like me!" I said thumbing myself in the chest. And I believe they did. We probably all loved Jesus one as much as the other . . . which was not at all, because none of us had any idea about who He was supposed to be, or how you could love somebody you couldn't see or who maybe wasn't even there.

I don't think I convinced The Preacher Boy that I really did love Jesus. I think he was just trying to convince me that I didn't. One thing I knew for sure—I was not The Preacher Boy!

On another occasion, I saw him heading in my direction and flipped my cigarette away. I didn't want to give him any reason to start on me again. But he caught it and walked right up to me,

"I saw you do that!" he confronted.

"Saw me do what?" I assumed a bewildered look.

"Flip that cigarette away," he replied. I said nothing.

"Why did you do that?" he pressed the issue.

"I was done with it."

"It looked to me like you had just lit it up."

I hung my head, and said

"I don't know why I threw it away,"

But the preacher boy knew why. He looked hard at me,

"You don't feel comfortable smoking around me do you?"

"No," I confessed. Boy! What was with this interrogation? Who did he think he was anyway?

"How would you feel if it was Jesus who came down the street instead of me?" So that's who he thought he was. He thought he was up there with Jesus.

"How would I know?" I asked, somewhat angry at the question.

"Someday you will be standing in front of Him instead of me—you'd better be ready when that day comes," he warned.

"How do you do that?" I asked, surprised at myself.

"Don't you know that God doesn't want you smoking?" he quarried.

"YES!" I said, more to be rid of him than anything else. I had had about enough of this.

"There! I said it! OK? I KNOW GOD DOESN'T WANT ME SMOKING!!"

"Well, that would be a good place to start getting ready." He turned and walked away as if he thought he had given me a clue to the puzzle of life and was leaving me to figure the rest out on my own.

Great! I guess that meant I had to quit smoking to escape hell. Well then, I was as good as damned. I had already tried and I knew I couldn't do it. This was a no-win situation.

My mind went back to my younger days and to the community center restroom where I had once tried to bum a cigarette off an older boy.

"I'm not going to give you one," he said. "You just waste them. You don't inhale."

That really dented my ego. So I threw what little bit of a chest I had out and demanded,

"Oh yeah? Gimme one and I'll show ya!"

He did. I lit it up and took the first drag, which I tried to take into my lungs. About halfway down my esophagus, it stopped dead. I felt as if someone had grabbed me by the throat and ripped my windpipe right out of my neck. I began to cough and choke. The older boy started laughing.

I couldn't have that, so I took another puff with the same effect. The boy's laughter, which by now had increased in volume and delight, seemed to be a good way off. The room was spinning around and there was a loud buzzing in my ears. If I looked like I felt I was probably turning green.

A third time I tried and still gagged as I fell against the trash can then to the floor. I can still hear the boy laughing as he went out the door, the clicking of his heels echoing down the hallway and his laughter fading off into the distance as he walked away.

I made up my mind I was never going to be embarrassed like that again. Every time I lit up thereafter I tried to inhale. At first, the result was the same. I think my body was trying to tell me something; *this was abnormal*. But I was determined and kept trying. It eventually became easier. Then I started bragging to my friends,

"Hey! I'm starting to inhale now!" as if it was like advancing to the next grade in school. Of course, they couldn't let me be getting ahead of them so they would always reply with,

"Yeah man, me too!"

Finally, the abnormal become the new normal for me. Inhaling was what I did. I even learned to show off by *French inhaling*, sticking out my lower lip and letting the smoke go out of my mouth as I breathed it up into my nose, and by blowing smoke rings.

Within a year, I decided I had done all the inhaling and clever tricks that I wanted to so I was going to quit smoking forever. I drug Terry Thrash into the deal with me. He and I tore a pack of cigarettes in two and ground them to powder under our feet to seal our covenant. That was at sundown. Before the next morning's sun came up we had both already broke our pledge, desperately scrounging around for cigarette butts. I couldn't even make it overnight. I tried again the next year and didn't make it an hour. What a difference inhaling had made. The abnormal had become the normal and now the normal had become the necessary. So if giving up smoking was what it took to be ready to stand before Jesus like the Preacher Boy said I was going to someday, then I was done for.

Though I was wrestling with issues that might have made me vulnerable to The Preacher Boy's appeals, watching him led me to conclude that he was paying a rather steep price for his faith; steeper than I felt I could ever pay. For one thing, everybody made fun of him, though he seemed to care little about it. Once it was known that the wild and wooly Ronnie was no longer the terror he had been, some went so far as to pick on him. If being a Christian meant I had to be as aggressive as he was about his faith, yet as passive as he was about how others treated him, I couldn't see myself ever fitting the role.

Not many days after Ronnie reproved me for smoking I saw him get between two boys who were fighting. They kept going at it anyway, so he got on his knees between them and begged them to stop. When one of them tried to get away, Ronnie clung to him. Then he began to pray vehemently for them both. Finally, the boys got fed up and both turned on him and began beating him. That someone would take a beating for their faith impressed me.

I am also sure The Preacher Boy was praying for me; probably fasting too for he believed in it. That may explain some of the things that were going through my mind in those days. I found myself praying most nights before I went to bed. I can only remember one thing for which I asked:

"God, help me to be a good Christian."

I was so ignorant about anything even resembling religion that I remember asking myself as I crawled into bed after the prayer,

What in the world is a Christian? How would I even know if my prayer was answered?

Then it occurred to me that a Christian must be someone who by some means unknown to me had the closest possible connection with God–if there was one. I was sure that if there was a real Christian in the world it had to be The Preacher Boy. I admired him and wished I could be like him, but for the life of me, could not imagine how a person would get there. These nighttime prayers went on only for a short while then stopped. I don't know why. But I do know that if Ronnie was praying for my conversion it was something he never got the pleasure of seeing.

The Preacher Boy did get through to me on one thing, though; it was the taking of God's name in vain. I mean–what if he was right? What if there was a God. Now I wasn't going to spend a lot of time trying to get on the good side of someone I wasn't sure was there. But it couldn't hurt to avoid getting on His bad side. What if I was going to meet Him some day? If it ever did happen maybe He'd go easy on me about the smoking if at least I hadn't done the name thing. It sounded like a pretty good compromise to me. Thereafter I rarely if ever treated God's name irreverently.

About 6 months after coming to know Ronnie Garlow Mom, Dad and I moved to Columbus, Ohio, leaving him and everyone else I knew behind. There I deepened my involvement in drugs and my interest in gang life. It was while we were there that Dad went on one of his prolonged drinking binges, only he never returned from this one. About a year later Mom and I moved back to her hometown, Zanesville, Ohio probably for the support of family. Even in the large city of Columbus, I didn't fit in well except with the few who chose to share my lifestyle, but in the small city of Zanesville, I was absolutely ridiculous. My usual dress was a black leather choker chain be–dangled motorcycle jacket that had a large spider painted on the back with the word Tarantula arched over it, along with blue jeans. Motorcycle boots completed the outfit. The few friends I did manage to make in Zanesville tried to help me with some brotherly advice.

"Max," they would say, "The way you dress and act might be alright for a large inner city but you can't act that way here. It won't work. You need to change a little."

I guess I wasn't changing fast enough to suit them so when David Wilkerson, the street gang evangelist from New York City of *The Cross and The Switchblade* fame, came to town there was a concerted effort on the part of my friends to get me into his meeting. Not that they were religious you understand, or anything like it. I believe that they just thought—*God certainly couldn't do Max any harm.* I'm sure they hoped the preacher or someone might say something that would help wake me up. When I heard that some of the young men with him would be telling their stories of street gang involvement I agreed to go.

The boy's stories proved to be every bit as spine tingling and blood curdling as I had anticipated. Each of them ended their talk by telling how God had changed them. One of those I heard that night was Nicky Cruz. After the stories, the preacher stepped forward and spoke a few moments after which he got us all on our feet. I thought that he was getting ready to let us go. Instead, he did something totally unexpected—at least by me.

"I want us all to bow our heads and close our eyes," He said. Most of us did. I know because I only half did.

He spoke again,

"If you were touched by these young men's *testimonies* tonight and felt God speaking to your heart I urge you to make a decision for Christ right now."

There was Ronnie Garlow's word! Testimony! What was this? A conspiracy? These guys didn't even know Ronnie. How did they know the way in which he used that word? What were they trying to prove? Testimonies were for courtrooms. Nobody was on trial here. Or were they? Regardless, I was, as Preacher Wilkerson put it, touched by the stories.

"You can spend eternity with Jesus forever in Heaven," I thought of the lake of fire on the other end of the chart that Lester had shown me; the preacher continued. "If you would like to be ready to stand before the Lord when your time comes, you can do it by becoming a Christian tonight. If you would like to be a Christian I want you to indicate it by raising your hand."

I don't know what got into me. Caught up in the moment I suppose. I sure didn't want to go to hell—if there was one. Anyway, next thing I knew my hand was high in the air, along with many others. I had forgotten all about my doubts about the spirit world and what those doubts had led me to believe. The preacher went on,

"Now I want all of you who raised your hands to come up front here. I want to pray the sinner's prayer with you."

That was the precise moment at which my friend Joe, who had talked me into being there in the first place, brought me back to reality by elbowing me in the ribs.

"Go on up Max, you raised your hand," he smirked, "you said you wanted to be a Christian."

What was he talking about? I looked up. Sure enough! There it was! My hand held high in the air. What was that traitor doing up there? I pulled it back down in a hurry and watched as several dozen others filed down the aisle. I stood my ground.

"Come ahead. Step right out into the aisle and come down to the front of the auditorium," the preacher was still coaxing.

Once grouped in front of the stage, he had them all bow their heads while he prayed for them. Most of the other people in the auditorium also had their heads bowed. As the preacher prayed a number of those up front began sobbing out loud.

They seem serious about this, I thought. *Maybe I'd better pray too–in case there is something to it,* so I bowed my head to join the praying. Just then, the preacher asked those down front to repeat after him while he said the sinner's prayer. They did so, line after line, telling God they were sorry for their sins, which they were willing to turn from and asking Jesus to come into their hearts. I repeated after him but I wasn't about to risk any further ridicule from Joe, so I did it in my mind. After the preacher was done praying he asked those down front,

"How many feel better now?"

Most of them either raised their hands or nodded their heads in the affirmative. It all confused my already befuddled mind. I had prayed in my seat just in case there was something to it but I hadn't felt bad in the first place and I certainly didn't feel any better now, which made me wonder if these people were self-deluded.

"Would any of you like to share a *testimony*?" the preacher asked. There it was again, *testimony*! Several did say something but I couldn't hear them. One young man must have said something impressive because the preacher asked him to come to the platform and repeat it into the microphone so the audience could hear him.

The teen talked about how he should have known better than to live like he had been. He declared that if there was satisfaction to be found in sin certainly these former gang members who had given their *testimony* would have found it. The youth, therefore, said he had rededicated his life back to Christ and was going to live right and be a *testimony* for Him.

Whatever. I didn't get it. Just like before. In the end, it all seemed to come down to a simple matter of emotions.

While the crusade did not affect me like my friends had hoped, my persona did slowly begin to change, not because they suggested it; that usually worked in reverse on me, but because there were no street gangs around for me to interact with. I continued to read all I could find about them but the fascination slowly began to wear off.

On top of that, a new focus began to compete for my attention. For the first time in my life, I took an interest in popular music. I think the *British Invasion,* which was going on at that time was what kick-started the interest in me. But as I was with words so I became with music; I could not be content just listening, I had to make those sounds myself. Accordingly, I began to teach myself how to play my Uncle Carl's acoustic Gibson guitar. I had an acquaintance at school that played in a band and he volunteered to show me a few things. One evening in the early fall he stopped by my uncle's place, catching me sitting with the guitar on the wooden steps in the rear of the apartment building. I immediately surrendered the instrument up to him and he stood with one foot on the stairs and the other on the ground, the raw porch light glaring down on him like a spotlight on a stage. He showed me how to play all the latest hits with such ease and dexterity that I was completely captivated. After that night, I was hooked, I had to learn how to do that myself.

By the next spring, Mom and I had moved back to Akron, birthplace of the rubber industry, Alcoholics Anonymous and rock and roll; in that order. The rubber industry was of no consequence to me but I could have used Alcoholics Anonymous if I had only known they existed.

But rock and roll did have my attention. I no longer had a guitar to work with since I had to leave my uncles behind in Zanesville, but my passion was so strong that until I could lay hold of one I took a piece of rolled up newspaper, flattened it out into the shape of a guitar neck, drew frets and strings on it and used it to practice chord changes as I played along with records. By the time I finally did land a guitar, I was so desperate that I played it until there was blood on the strings. By this means, I preoccupied myself to such a level that I made no connection with former gang members. Though Lester had never been part of the street gangs even he and I drifted apart as I began to acquire a new set of friends whose interests lay in music.

Even so, I continued to have an issue with drinking, and it was by drinking that I soon went through one of the most shameful experiences of my life. The next morning sitting on the edge of my bed still feeling the effects of the night before, I realized how absolutely sick I was of my whole life. I detested what both it and I had become. I wanted to change but I was helpless to do it. I didn't know how to become anything different much less anything better. For that matter, I didn't even know what something better might look like.

Thoughtlessly I reached up and turned the radio on. Seemingly out of nowhere a preacher was speaking. I had never heard a preacher on that station before. He was saying that thousands of years ago, the Bible foretold of things that were happening around us right now every day and that it was one of the best *testimonies* that the Bible was written by God. There was that word again! *Testimony!*

Then a thought flitted through my mind.

The Bible! The preacher said that God, Himself wrote it. Maybe that's it! Maybe it can tell me what I'm looking for! For the first time in a long time, I felt hope again spring up within me.

I went to my mother's closet and got a box down from the top shelf. Digging through its contents I found on the bottom the Bible Mom carried with her everywhere we moved. She never read it. She used it to store things in; a lock of someone's hair, a baby picture of one of my cousins, a newspaper photograph of a flood in the old hometown and a pressed flower. I returned to the edge of my bed with the Bible in hand and began reading, looking for a life–changing message. I started reading it just like you would any other book, at the beginning. It read:

"In the beginning God created the heavens and the earth. And the earth was without form and void and darkness was upon the face of the deep."

OK so far so good. I read on about creation, and man's disobedience.

Well, I already know I've disobeyed and I'm in a mess, I thought. *Where is the part that tells me how to change?*

Several chapters later I ran into the *begats:* So and so begat so and so who begat so and so; so on and so forth.

I got through the first short wave of them in chapter four. But then came what appeared to be the main event in chapter five. It seemed to go on forever. So and so begat so and so, who begat so and so; it was endless. Somehow, I managed to get through that. Then came the real marathon in chapter ten. I couldn't even pronounce most of these names. I had reached my limit. My interest and hope dropped down dead right there in the middle of chapter ten.

Now just how relevant is that? I sarcastically asked myself. It seemed to me that if the purpose of the book was to tell me how to change my life it ought to at least mention it somewhere near the beginning not bury it deep within its pages.

Maybe if I had someone to explain it to me, I thought. *Maybe then I could make some sense of it,* but there was nobody.

I didn't know what had become of Ronnie Garlow, and the only other person I was aware of who knew anything about the Bible was my literature teacher at school. He showed up drunk or hung over most of the time and he had the disposition of a badger to go with it. Still, he declared that the Bible was beautiful literature and that he loved to read it. We should read it too he suggested. But he never said anything about it being a *testimony* or telling how it could change somebody's life. Besides, his life seemed to need a good deal of changing itself. I concluded that if he, with all his education, hadn't found the message in the Bible that I was hoping for, then, how could I? I didn't have a chance. *Maybe there wasn't any message.* Well, it was a good thought anyway, but there was far too much in that book for me to wade through and try to make sense out of.

So, I reverently closed the Bible and returned it to its place at the bottom of the box, which I placed back on the top shelf of Mom's closet. Eventually, the remorse wore off and life was good again–for now: but my entire worldview was about to receive a mighty shaking.

CHAPTER 4

ONE STEP BEYOND

It was a quiet summer evening in 1965. A cool breeze was wafting through the air. The sun had already slipped behind the horizon; its last glorious rays painting tints of gold and red on the blue canvas of the sky and gilding the edges of the pillowing gray clouds.

By now several of us from our east side neighborhood had formed a rock band, naming ourselves *Justus*. We had spent the first part of this particular evening jamming. Now, as we sat around the room, we could see twilight descending upon the world through the window to the west.

The shadows of the trees that had grown long during the setting of the sun now disappeared altogether, consumed by the gathering darkness. Soon the yellow glow from a lone streetlamp up the court beamed like a distant beacon through the haze of a fog that had risen from the earth. It was then that the crescent moon came out and sailed upon its' cloudy sea creating a perfect aura for what happened next.

We started telling scary stories, as the young are prone to do, each one of us trying to outdo the last. Finally, our new drummer Reggie spoke up,

"Hey! I know what. Do you guys want to do something *really* different?"

"What's that?" someone asked.

"Let's have a séance."

"What? What's that?" Al asked.

"It's where you call someone up from the dead," Reggie explained.

"Now how can you do that?" Rick asked skeptically.

"Well, when someone dies apparently his or her spirit is still around. I guess it's just on the other side. But you can communicate with them. You can call them back into this world," Reggie said.

"You mean you can raise someone from the dead?" Dave asked with a scowl on his face.

"No," Reggie said, "What you do is you call their spirit back and talk with it. My parents do it all the time."

Neither Rick nor I believed in any such thing as an afterlife. We had long before decided that there was nothing more to life than this material, physical world. We took pride in calling ourselves atheists. But neither of us said anything.

Why bother? I figured. *They'll find out soon enough when nothing happens.* In the meantime, I decided to just watch and see what took place. After all, it was interesting. This certainly wasn't your everyday experience.

"Well, how do you 'talk' with these spirits?" Rick inquired.

"We'll need a table," Reggie said.

"Like what?" I asked. "We've got one in the kitchen."

"No, something smaller that we can bring in here. Something like a game table," he said.

"The only thing we have like that would be the coffee table in the living room," I suggested.

"That'll work," he said.

I took Dave into the living room where my mother and stepfather were watching television. We picked up the coffee table and carried it out of the room with my parents' heads slowing turning as they watched wondering what we were up to now.

After we put the table in the center of my room Reggie had us all gather around it, some sitting on chairs, me on the night table and others on the edge of the bed. Reggie instructed us to each put both hands on the table in front of us, crossing our thumbs over each other. He then had us cross our little fingers with the person on either side of us creating a circuit all the way around the table. Then we turned out the light, which since the sun by now had gone down, left us sitting in the dark.

"Who has someone they would like to talk to?" Reggie asked.

"My grandmother died a couple of years ago," Dave said. "I miss her. I would like to hear from her if it can be done."

Reggie continued,

"Let's all concentrate on Dave's grandmother. What was her name, Dave?"

"Helen," Dave answered.

And with that, we all began concentrating on Helen.

"Repeat after me," Reggie instructed us.

"Rise table rise, rise table rise, rise table rise . . ."

We all chanted it over and over like a funeral dirge. It was almost hypnotic.

I honestly didn't expect anything to happen but then it did happen–the event that changed my life–forever. Suddenly I became aware of a very real presence seeping into the room, rising as stealthily as the fog outside had recently risen, seemingly out of nowhere. I carefully opened my eyes though I wasn't supposed to and saw by what little light the street lamp up the court shone in through the window, a thick gray mist over the entire room. It was somewhat like the fog outside in appearance, only dry.

Presently the table began to tremble and shake. Then it slowly reared up on two of its legs. I could hardly believe my senses. I looked under the table to see if there wasn't some type of trickery; if these guys weren't pulling or lifting somehow on the table. I saw that they were not. What's more, I knew that this was my room and my table. It was certain that there were no strings attached. The table stood quivering almost as if it were flesh. Then Reggie spoke,

"Let's thank Jesus for coming here among us tonight," to which we all replied,

"Thank you, Jesus."

Now that threw me a curve. What did Jesus have to do with this? We were trying to contact Helen, not Jesus. Where was she? Reggie began talking with—I guess the spirit of Jesus. To communicate with this presence, he would ask it, or him, yes and no questions. If the table went all the way down and tapped the floor then rose again to its former position, the answer was yes, if it only went half way to the floor the answer was no.

"Is David's Grandmother Helen over on your side?"

The table went down. It hit the floor and returned to its former place.

"Is she able to come and talk to us here tonight?"

Again, the table struck the floor indicating that she could.

"Would you call for her now?"

Once again, the table hit the floor. Then Reggie sat up straight as if straining to hear something.

"I feel another presence coming into the room," he announced.

"Jesus, is Helen here with us now?"

Again the table thumped the floor.

"Grandma!" David exclaimed, "Are you ok?"

The response was "Yes"

"Are you in any pain or hurting at all?"

At this question, the table dropped only half way to the floor then stopped and rose again indicating that she was not hurting.

David continued talking with his grandmother. Now and then Reggie would interrupt to ask a question about things that were going on in the spirit world. Then Dave, apparently to satisfy his curiosity, asked a trick question,

"Grandma, if this is really you could you tap the floor for how many trips we made to Wyoming as I was growing up?"

That must have ticked Helen off because Dave immediately screamed and was thrown into what appeared to be a seizure. Instantly our conversation with Helen was ended. We turned on the light and found Dave lying on his back on the bed, his face twisted and contorted as he trembled and shook. We were all gathered around shouting his name and shaking him trying to bring him to his senses. Reggie spotted a tear running down his face.

"Look!" he declared, "It's formaldehyde!"

I highly doubted it. While I couldn't deny that something beyond my ability to explain was happening, I still couldn't let it get me to call what was obviously a simple tear, formaldehyde.

This guy's imagination is running away with him, I thought.

Slowly Dave calmed down and regained consciousness.

"Wha— what happened?" he asked.

"We don't know!" Rick ventured.

"I think you got Helen mad," Reggie said with assurance.

"You can't question these spirits on who they say they are. They get real sensitive about it." He explained. "By the way, how many trips to Wyoming did you two make together?"

"None," Dave sheepishly confessed.

"Well, there it is. You were trying to get the upper hand in the conversation. They don't like that. Was she by any chance epileptic?"

"Why, yes she was," Dave admitted.

"It must have been her spirit that seized you," Reggie concluded.

"Wow! Let's do it again!" Al suggested.

By now there was no way that we weren't going to do it again. We had two more séances without any negative incidents that evening. When Lester Lowe with a couple of friends stopped by we tried to show them what we had been doing, but it wouldn't work. Yet as soon as they were gone, we tried again and it did.

Following that séance, we began comparing our thoughts.

"This is great man! These things don't show themselves to just anyone. But they are showing themselves to us," said Dave.

"I wonder why?" Al asked.

"Who cares?" was Rick's response. Then he asked Reggie, "What other kinds of things do these spirits do?"

"Like what?" Reggie asked.

"I mean things like give you power over other people," Rick explained himself.

"Well, I have heard of them giving people the ability to read minds. I think I've heard something about the power to heal too," Reggie said.

"What about persuasive power? Like getting people to do things?" Dave asked.

"Yeah, I've heard of that sort of thing," Reggie answered. "They would call that a spell."

"Can they tell the future?" was my question.

"Oh yes," Reggie was absolute, "they usually do that through someone. They call it fortune telling."

"How about sending them after someone? You know, like to get even," Rick asked.

"Commonly known as a curse," Reggie explained.

It was Al who made the suggestion that seemed to be running through several of our minds.

"Look guys, do you have any idea how much of a privilege we have here? If the rest of the world doesn't know about these things, what makes us so special that they would show themselves to us?"

"Maybe we are specially chosen?" suggested Dave.

"It has to be more than coincidence that we are gathered here tonight just as we are. It must have been in the books. You know—meant to be," I added.

"Whooooa!" said Rick as if he had just received an epiphany. "Imagine if we could get these spirits to do things for us."

"Wouldn't that be kinda like using them?" Dave asked.

"Yes," Rick answered dubiously, "but, why shouldn't we? They chose us. They're probably here to help us accomplish something."

Al spoke up,

"Yeah, and if we can get them to work for us with nobody else realizing what was happening, people would play right along."

Reggie seemed to be getting a little concerned about the direction this conversation was taking. It was his turn to ask a question.

"And what kind of things are we talking about getting them to motivate others to do?"

"Whatever!" Al answered. "Such as giving us fame and fortune."

"Yeah and how about a recording contract!" said Rick.

"What about power over the crowds!" Dave added.

My mind began to draw its own picture of us performing in front of thousands of screaming fans, and power flowing through us to them. I even saw people getting healed of sicknesses, and us eventually gaining political status through the influence of these unseen powers. A true euphoria began to settle down over me.

For most of us, Reggie being the one exception, this was the only supernatural manifestation we had ever seen. For all any of us knew this was God. None of us had ever felt a presence like this before. It was our first contact with anything like it.

I felt as if we were sallying forth into a life–long adventure. It was like we had made the greatest discovery imaginable; as if we had stumbled upon the curtain that separated us from some other world. Certainly, no scientist, inventor, or explorer ever felt a keener sense of thrill after a grand discovery than I did that night. Above all, I was sure that we were destined for greatness. How it was to be achieved I did not know. One thing was certain; it was all connected to these supernatural beings. It was up to them to reveal our destiny and it was up to us to follow. They would lead us up the ladder to fame, success, power and fortune.

Of course, I had my apprehensions. I am after all; both blessed and cursed with a cautious nature. But there appeared to be no danger here. Even when they later began acting fiendish I thought it worth the risk if we could milk out of these entities what we wanted. In my naiveté, I even wondered if they might not, in the order of things, be subject to our commands.

While none of what I experienced that night fit with anything I had ever heard or thought about a supernatural world, one thing was for sure; there was no denying that this was real.

Over the next several months, we began meeting nightly to have more séances. In the end, our gatherings developed into a full–blown, home–brewed religion. If you have further interest in this part of the story you can read more about it in book one of the *Believe It or Not Series: The Gates of Hell.*

Then came the day in October of that year when we had our final séance. It was precipitated by a friend who I told about our meetings, and he had spread throughout the apartment building he lived in, that I insisted my group and I had fallen upon a portal to the spirit world. Thereafter the normally accepting social network of the building was at best skeptical, and at worst downright antagonistic.

Several of us, sitting in my friends' living room on that October afternoon were locked in the conversational doldrums of a stalemated dispute. Phrases such as 'mass hysteria' and 'overactive imaginations' were being flung about, which was bad enough but when someone threw down the word 'crazy', I took it as the gauntlet of a challenge. The first two phrases were more group oriented, but crazy–that was personal. This bordered on insult.

Jumping to my feet, I declared,

"OK, that's it! It's time to put up or shut up! Tonight, after the sun goes down I want everybody in this building out on the front porch. I'm going to bring my friends over here and we'll prove to you that this thing is real. We're going to have a séance!"

That evening after sunset, my friends and I assembled at the appointed place. The people began to gather around as we brought a small table out from one of the apartments. By the time we began everyone in the building was present. We soon made our contact and the table rose into the air. Some of the people gasped and backed off. Others bewildered leaned in to examine the table. We ignored them and continued with our séance as if they weren't present.

For several weeks, I had had a growing hunch in the back of my mind that seemed to come to full term that evening. Feeling strangely impressed to ask a question based on the hunch I inquired,

"Are we doing something we shouldn't be doing?"

The table dipped to the floor, hit it and rose again indicating that we were.

Now, I decided, was the time to play my suspicion out to the full. So, I asked a second question,

"Would we be best off if we would let you go and never call you up again?"

Once more the table signified a *yes* by dropping to the floor and striking it. I do not pretend to understand, what appears to be an illogical move on the part of the spirits, of divulging such information. What I do know is that sometimes their strategy involves more than what is readily seen on the surface. Looking at the surprised faces of those sitting around the table I acted as spokesman for us all, with or without their approval I said,

"All right– this is the last séance we're ever going to hold. But before you go I want you to convince everybody on this porch that you are a reality–send a scent of roses so strong that nobody here will doubt your existence."

With that the table went down, the presence withdrew, and a scent of roses came flooding and tumbling over the porch.

Those present "oohed and aahed." Everybody there acknowledged the authenticity of what they had just witnessed.

Perhaps the story from this point on would have been different had I not asked for the parting favor of the rose scent. My final request seemed to grant the departing spirit an open door through which it and his cohorts could freely return.

Immediately after this séance my friends and I decided to take a walk around the block. We weren't ten yards away from the spot where we had decided to never have another séance, and it wasn't ten minutes after we had made the decision, when for the first time, after months of involvement with the spirit world, one of those presences began to settle down over us when we had not asked for it to come. In fact, we didn't want it to be there—but we couldn't stop it or get rid of it.

I don't know about the others. I can't tell what kind of an impression was made upon them. I can only say that after the experience, we were all using the same adjectives to describe it.

I experienced an extreme sense of anxious foreboding. I could sense something that I couldn't hide from looking at me from every direction. I couldn't see it, but I could perceive it! It was just beyond my fingertips as if I could reach out and touch it. Suddenly I was aware that it was right behind me. I felt its hot breath breathing down my neck. I quickly turned to face my enemy. There was nobody there. But I still felt it right behind me. I turned again. No one. I sensed the very essence of evil in the atmosphere. It was so devilish, so hellish, and so demonic that the horror of its invisible nearness struck terror into my heart. I looked down and saw that my arm was covered with goose bumps with its hair standing almost straight out.

Suddenly, and I can't explain this, I became aware that the diabolical fiend was seeping into me. Immediately my will rose up against its entrance. It stopped. I think it had to.

But then I experienced a tremendous sense of pressure. The presence pressed down on every square inch of my being. It was almost physical. It was as if it was trying to force its way in against my will. It wanted to take over.

Something snapped inside of me and I went whooping and hollering down the street like a maniac, jumping and spinning with arms flailing wildly in every direction animated by whatever it was that had taken hold of me. I danced into the circle of light from a streetlamp and kicked the pole with all my might, jamming my entire foot which immediately brought me back to my senses.

We all spent that night together at the apartment building. It was passed with wave after wave of spirit attacks assailing us. We kept each other awake for fear these supernatural beings would enter into us while sleeping.

We began spending all our nights together. We would sleep in the daytime when the spirits seemed to be much less active and needed less warding off. If by chance, we did fall off to sleep during one of our nighttime vigils more times than not we were awakened by a terrifying presence coming into the room and filling our hearts with pure fear.

Then things would begin to happen. Pictures would be torn from the wall and thrown to the floor. Objects would get up of their own accord and float through the air. Voices would speak out of nowhere. Lights would turn themselves off and on. Footsteps would run across the floor so heavy that it would rattle the windows in the wall, but there would be no one there. These and other like phenomena occurred with regularity.

Walking into one of the cloud–like presences that seemed to float around at will, as we made our way down the street at night, was such a tangible experience that it was akin to walking into a brick wall.

We would come into contact with people who obviously had these spirits in them. Their eyes would glow a strange iridescent green and flash with unexplainable hatred when they saw us. We called it the *possessed glare*. Such individuals seemed to be everywhere. We would run into them at parties, in stores and restaurants, or on the street. A few times these spirits blatantly threatened us speaking directly through someone.

It is an understatement to say that we were terrified. In our desperation, Rick and I looked Reggie up and explained to him how out of control things had become.

Reggie informed us that our experience wasn't all that unusual. He said that he wasn't deeply enough involved to know why it happens, but he had learned from both experience and his parents that these spirits were subject to the name of Jesus. Though it made no sense to me why they would be subject to one name more than another, I was desperate enough to try anything. I knew that there was supposed to be something special about the name of Jesus, maybe something magical was more along the line of my thinking. We asked if he could show us how it worked.

"Sure," Reggie offered. "Come over to my place this evening. If the spirits start acting up like you say they have been, I'll get a chance to show you."

That night we met at Reggie's house. Shortly after our arrival, the spirits indicated their presence by flickering the lights off and on a number of times. Reggie had us stand in a circle and hold hands. He then told us to repeat after him as he began to chant the name of Jesus over and over so rapidly that we were slurring the words together,

"Jesus, Jesus, Jesus, Jesus, Jesus, Jesus, Jesus, Jesus . . ," we chanted dozens of times. It almost reminded me of the "rise table rise" incantations Reggie had taught us before. To me, it was about the same thing as the devotees of Vishnu chanting "Hare Krishna, Hare Krishna, Krishna Hare, Hare Krishna," I couldn't believe that this was me doing this. I felt stupid if not downright embarrassed.

Eventually, things did begin to calm down. But then they eventually always did. Maybe the name of Jesus did help some. If it did, it wasn't very dramatic. I was unresolved enough on the matter that I decided to reserve judgment for the time being.

The next evening as I sat alone in my bedroom, I felt that familiar presence enter into my room. But something happened that night that caught me off guard and I am sure the spirit as well. It happened with absolutely no effort on my part. It was as if something grabbed me by the nape of the neck and jerked me straight up on my feet. I addressed the spirit directly, authoritatively declaring,

"I rebuke you in the name of Jesus!"

I was shocked. It was almost as if someone else had spoken it through me. I had no idea where the phrase had even come from. But I can tell you this; instantly all paranormal activity stopped dead. I could almost hear the spirit screaming,

"Where did you find out about that name?"

I felt the presence leave; no, more accurately I felt it flee from the room. I stood there numb and amazed. I couldn't believe what had just taken place.

In a few minutes, I sensed the spirit coming back into the room. It was as if it were peeking out from around the corner saying,

"What hit me?" But I was ready this time. I had a weapon. I yelled it out again,

"I rebuke you in the name of Jesus!" Again, as quickly as I said it the presence was gone.

Knowing that the name Jesus came from the Bible I Immediately made a trip to my mother's closet and got the box with the Bible in it down from the top shelf again.

Taking the Bible into the kitchen I laid it on its spine on the table and let it fall open. At once, my eyes fell upon Psalm 7. I began to read from what I thought was pronounced The Book of Palms. It read,

"*Oh Lord my God in you do I put my trust.*" That verse immediately brought God to my attention. In all our searching for deliverance from the spirits, we had never considered God as a source of help. I knew for sure now that there was a spirit world with evil beings in it. Maybe the Christians were onto something. I also knew that it would be great if there were a God. I could certainly use His help now. I read on,

"*Save me from all them that persecute me, and deliver me:*" I knew I needed to be delivered. These spirits and maybe the devil himself were hot on my trail. I continued to read on.

"*Lest he tear my soul like a lion, rending it in pieces.*"

I knew that a physical enemy could tear my body but only a spiritual enemy could tear my soul. So I knew that the lion spoken of was figurative for a spiritual enemy. Furthermore, it said, lest 'he' tear my soul, rather than 'they'. Was this a confirmation that there was a single mastermind behind all of this?

"Where are these thoughts coming from?" I wondered to myself.

Suddenly and unexpectedly I was aware of another kind of presence in the room. I had been so engrossed in my reading that it had snuck up on me. Like the air in the room, it was everywhere and mirrored the book I held in my hand. It was as if the presence was flowing from or through its words. It was akin to reading a book then looking up and there, standing before you, is its author, magically transported into your presence. I did, in fact, look up, and around, but there was no one there. At that very moment, a self-authenticating impression, which under any other circumstance I might have called a more highly developed intuition, came into my mind. It was so clear it might as well have been an audible voice.

"Read on, I'll help you understand," It said.

I delved back into the book like a starving man into a platter of food.

As I read the rest of the chapter I found God promising protection to whoever wrote this "*Palm.*" Though his enemy had dug a pit to ensnare the writer, the antagonist himself was going to fall into it. Then his violent dealings were going to come crashing down upon the villain's own head.

After reading the Psalm, following yet another impression, I pushed back the chair I was sitting on and knelt beside the table. This was the first time in my life I had ever prayed an intelligent sincere prayer. I asked God to protect me.

The invisible presence around me grew stronger as I prayed. And yes, it was a presence, as were the others I had come to know, but of a completely different essence. This one I knew I could trust. There was no drawing back in fear. It was a bright, delectable presence that produced an extreme sense of delight and joy within me. Never before had I experienced such an awareness of acceptance and confirmation.

In a few moments, it subsided, then it returned again, only stronger. Again, it abated but then returned stronger yet. Over and over it came, each time the presence more pungent than before until it was nearly overwhelming. It was like standing on the shoreline of an infinite ocean of love with wave after wave crashing over me. Perhaps the best word for what I felt that night is-glory.

I didn't know if this was God for sure but it was what anyone would think God should be like. And that was good enough for me. I instinctively knew that this was what I was made for, this presence–this Spirit. Again that impression upon my inner person spoke,

"If you will, from this day forward, walk with me according to the best of your understanding I will protect you from these evil spirits."

There was nothing more. It sounded like a covenant. It was a promise–a promise of protection; exactly what I had requested. And it is a promise that has never failed me to this day. The tables had turned.

CHAPTER 5

INSTINITY!

What I experienced the night I first used the name of Jesus, read the Bible and prayed, was not any sort of an evangelical awaking. For one thing, I had no concept of sin and therefore could neither confess it nor repent of it. Just the same, it was a start. I began reading the Bible–religiously you might say, over the next year. My interest in it grew far beyond a passing whim. For me, it was a new book; not a reprint of some ancient document containing worn-out creeds that I had heard ever since childhood until they had lost their wonder. No, for me the Bible was a *living* book. There was no staleness in the story of Jesus as far as I was concerned. As I read the pages of the New Testament, it was as if Christ walked the earth again. God seemed to speak to me in every line. The marvel of the story grew on me until I became absolutely obsessed.

Having relayed my experience of using the name of Jesus and my encounter with God while reading the Bible to the other members of our band, they too now shared my passion for the Bible. The book of Revelation particularly appealed to us because it seemed pertinent to our times. We became convinced that we were in the last days and the human race was about to self–destruct. We were sure that being privy to such information had to bring with it a responsibility to forewarn others. And so it came to pass that we began calling ourselves *Warners*. *Justus* was *who* we were; *Warners* was *what* we were. As a result, the original songs our group played now took on an apocalyptic tone.

Still, we knew that we were ill–informed on most of the Bible's meaning. When you've never read anything but Modern English, you don't just pick the King James Bible up, nearly the only one available in those days, and get doctrine out of it. I was the only member of our band that had any background in literature, and while having read Shakespeare and other works from the seventeenth century may have put me ahead of my friends when it came to an understanding of Early Modern English, even I struggled with much of what we found in the pages of Sacred Writ.

So where do you go when you want help understanding the Bible? To church of course! They are supposed to be the experts. And of course, everybody knows that bigger is better: right? Such was the line of reasoning that lead us to one of the largest churches in our part of town. We decided that the way to start our quest was by attending their public church services.

The first Sunday my friends and I walked in, they looked at us as if we had recently escaped from the local zoo and wished someone would round us up and put us back in our cages in a hurry. Cold welcome. I'm sure they thought we were there to start trouble, but that was the furthest thing from our minds. By the time we had attended the church for the biggest part of a month, we had heard the pastor, Dr. Harvey, mention a number of subjects that were of great interest to us, but the Sunday he spoke about the demonized man of Luke chapter 8 convinced us that we needed to have a talk with the Doctor to be sure we were safe in putting ourselves under his ministry. When it came to matters of truth, we had discovered that there was no room for exposing ourselves to the viruses of error. Much of what Dr. Harvey said on the occasion of the

Luke 8 sermon resonated with us, but there were nuances that made us wonder if he really believed the Bible. The greatest point of contention was when he purported Jesus to be a psychologist who was millenniums ahead of his time because he was able to cure this man, the demoniac, in a single session. Our question was that if all the changes that took place were inside the man's psyche, and if that was the only problem he had, then where did the entities that left him and entered into the pigs causing them to stampede into the sea fit in?

Rick and I decided to take our questions directly to the source by getting an interview with Dr. Harvey. We tried for several weeks before successfully scheduling a time to see him.

On the day of our meeting, we entered into the business wing of the church, approached the secretary and informed her that we were there for our appointment with Dr. Harvey. She pushed the button on the intercom that sat beside her phone.

"Your appointment is here Dr. Harvey." She announced.

"Tell them to have a seat, I'll be with them in a few minutes," we heard the intercom respond.

We sat off to the side for what seemed like a long time. Eventually, Dr. Harvey beeped and told the secretary to show us in.

Stepping into his study, we saw the good Doctor sitting in an overstuffed swivel chair behind a mahogany desk that was in the middle of the room. To his left was a large ceiling to floor window while the rest of the walls were lined with bookshelves, most of them loaded with not only with books, but with miniature elephants as well, some carved out of various materials, some cast, others made out of porcelain, and a few out of resin. There must have been over a hundred of them. Dr. Harvey was a tall plump man in his fifties who wore dark rimmed glasses and had straight black slicked back hair. Even in his office, he was wearing a clergy collar and garb. When his secretary ceremoniously announced us he rose from his chair and enthusiastically greeted us with hearty handshakes. You would have thought we were celebrities, or that he was running for some political office.

After the secretary exited we started with small talk, about the most notable thing in the room—elephants. Where had they all come from, what did they mean, and why so many? He informed us that he was a world traveler and lecturer. Africa was one of his frequent destinations.

"Lecture in Africa?" Rick was surprised, "Isn't that a bit over the people's heads?"

"Heaven's no young man," The Doctor leaned back in his chair, "Much of Africa is just like here. It's only outside the cities that it continues to be the Dark Continent it once was. In fact, even those in the jungles have a lot to teach us."

"Oh," Rick's eyes were roving all over the room.

"Anyway . . ," the Dr. arose from his seated position and walked around our chairs,

"I bought this particular elephant," he said as he stepped up to the shelf behind us and picked up one of the carved statues, "on a very early trip to Johannesburg. It was my first. After I bought several more . . ," He put the elephant down and walked over to the shelf on our right and picked up what looked to be a jade one "Including this one, which I picked up on my first tour in India," he held it up for us to see, "others seemed to catch on." He put the elephant down and headed back toward his seat.

"Now, whenever there is any sort of an occasion or I travel somewhere to speak I am always gifted with another elephant from some remote part of the world."

Then we inquired what his lectures were about; big mistake. He sat back down and launched off on a tirade about himself that I thought would never end. He told us of his many studies and travels and his philosophy of life. But it all weaved together as if it were a discourse. It was as if he were lecturing to an audience of two. He worked himself up into a crescendo after which he began the wrap up by describing the tombstone he had contracted with somebody in Europe to carve for him. By now he was on his feet again, this time illustrating as he described the picture that was engraved upon his monuments marble side. It was a representation of him in Swiss Alp garb climbing up the side of a mountain that had the sun setting over its summit. In the picture, he was leaning backward holding onto a rope with his head thrown back. He now himself was leaning back with his face turned up toward the top of the tall window beside his desk. Underneath the picture, he said there was a single word. And here he dramatically gesticulated widely with his hand as he said it,

"–YET!"

And there he stopped stone still with his upturned palm held high above his head toward the top of the window he was staring at.

He held his pose as if he were waiting for applause. In the uncomfortable silence I glanced questionably at Rick and he at me. Then without moving a muscle Dr. Harvey's eyes rolled down and looked at us out of his upturned face.

"And what can I do for you?" he asked as he fell out of his pose and back into his chair.

It was Rick who spoke up,

"We are Warners!"

A rather blunt approach I thought. But that was Rick.

"Warners? Who are you warning? And what about?"

"Have you ever read the book of Revelation in the Bible?" Rick asked.

"My dear boy! Of course I have, I'm a minister of the gospel," the doctor emphasized.

Rick continued, "We know that we are living in the time of the end and we have been sent by God to warn people about it."

"Oh. So you mean a bit like the Two Witnesses?" Doctor Harvey asked.

"Exactly!" Rick emphatically shook his head.

I broke in enthusiastically asking, "You know how people in the book of Revelation are seeing into the spirit world–seeing spiritual beings with their physical eyes, right?"

"I understand what you are saying." The doctor humored us.

"Well we have discovered, totally by accident that the demonic activity in the atmosphere is being stepped up. Even now some people are beginning to get glimpses into what is happening on the other side," I went on.

"And how did you find this out?" Dr. Harvey tilted his head like a Cocker Spaniel trying to understand.

"By a friend of ours having séances," Rick spoke up.

"But we decided to get out of that," I quickly explained.

"And that's when the demons got mad and turned on us!" Rick broke in. The intensity of our conversation was mounting.

"Now they're after us!" I declared. "Mad as can be. They are hot on our trail!" Our exchange was still gaining momentum.

"Breathing down our necks," Rick was now on his feet.

"But we found out that they are subject to the name of Jesus!" I pounded my fist on the desk to punctuate the name. "That has made them madder than ever and put us on the other side of the fence," Our dialogue was now reaching nigh unto fever pitch as if we had been waiting too long to tell someone official about all this.

"Now that we have discovered that they are the ones working behind the scenes pulling the strings somebody has to warn people before everything breaks loose!" Rick was nearly beside himself.

The further we went the more disturbed the expression on Dr. Harvey's face became. I finally slowed down and tried to get Rick to do the same.

"Rick," I tried to get his attention. He rattled on.

"Rick!" he wasn't even hearing me.

"Rick!" I grabbed his arm with both hands and shook it. He stopped in the middle of a sentence and looked at me.

"What?"

"Just a minute," I held my index finger straight up between us. Turning my attention to Dr. Harvey I asked,

"Is there something wrong?"

"Well yes," the doctor said, "since you asked. This is completely heathenistic," I stood in stunned silence. Shot down out of the sky in flames.

"What? Why's that?" Rick inquired.

"Because there isn't any devil." He answered.

"What?!" Rick and I echoed each other.

"You heard me. There isn't any devil."

"There isn't?" I scowled

"No!" He replied.

I turned my face toward Rick but kept my eyes on Dr. Harvey.

"Hey, Rick!"

"Yeah, man?"

Now I pulled my eyes away from the doctor and looked full in Rick's face.

"There ain't no devil!"

"There isn't?"

"No!"

"It's a good thing you told me because I'd have never known it."

I turned back to Dr. Harvey,

"What do you mean there isn't any devil? What do you call him?"

"Oh! Well, I understand why you boys are thinking like you are. There is an abstract force or power out there, but nothing personal. There isn't some kind of a scheming, planning, plotting, entity trying to trick us all and damn the world. What kind of a God would permit that?"

"Uh–the kind of a God the Bible talks about?" Rick challenged.

"Those my son were ideas from darker ages. Like what we have now in Africa or India."

"And what about where the Bible talks about satan?" I asked.

The Doctor immediately reverted to lecture mode.

"The Bible may be a contact point for us to meet God, but you can't take it at face value. All the devil is, is a myth. To get the real message of the Bible you have to demythologize it. What the devil represents is the collective evil in all of us."

If you've ever tried to talk someone out of the devil who's been in direct contact with him, you know what a job Dr. Harvey had on his hands. I knew that he wasn't going to convince me that the devil was a figment of my imagination. And it didn't seem very promising that we were going be able to talk him into the devil.

So I thought I'd change the subject to some more neutral ground. The thought of answered prayer came to mind. *That's something all Christians would agree on* I told myself. So as tactfully as I knew how–which wasn't very– I switched over to the subject of petition.

"Well . . . ahh . . . I . . . (ahem) . . . eh . . . heh . . . boy, the Lord sure has been answering prayer for us lately."

Dr. Harvey got that same troubled look on his face. No sense in hesitating now I decided.

"Now, what's wrong?" I stared at the Doctor.

"This is the height of ignorance! Don't you understand? God doesn't answer prayer!" I was shocked right out of my mind.

"He doesn't?"

"No!"

Once again, I turned my face toward Rick but kept my eyes on Dr. Harvey.

"Hey, Rick!"

"Yeah man?"

Now I pulled my eyes away from the Doctor and looked full in Rick's face.

"God doesn't answer prayer!"

"He doesn't?"

"Nope!"

"I'm glad you told me! I'd have never known it!"

I looked back to Dr. Harvey,

"What do you mean, God doesn't answer prayer?"

"Where did you get the idea that He did?" Dr. Harvey asked.

"It's public information!" Rick spouted off, "You find it in the Bible!" he stressed with rising emotions.

"Can't you understand?" The Doctor went on, "God made this world like a watchmaker makes a watch. He wound it up and sent it out of His world–making shop. It runs on its own. He doesn't have to intervene. Someday it may run down; if it does then He'll get involved. But until then–He doesn't!"

"Can you show me that in the Bible?" I asked.

"No. But why should I have to?"

"Because that's the source of information," I answered.

"Like I said, the Bible is just a book. A good one to be sure. But that's all it is. You know, editors putting together ancient documents that were based on myths that had been passed down for generations by word of mouth. Like I said you have to demythologize it to get at its real message."

"You know Doctor, a few months ago, I might have agreed with you," I rose to my feet to leave, "but I wouldn't have been doing it as a representative of God!"

I could easily see that whatever little spiritual ground my friends and I had gained we were light years ahead of Dr. Harvey. It suddenly occurred to me–I wondered if Providence might have planted the thought in my mind, that I had read somewhere in the Bible about people believing the '*doctrines of devils*' in the last days. I also remember there being something about '*spiritual wickedness in high places*' I had long ago learned that demons could be at work even when no one felt their presence. But could they actually plant ideas right into people's heads without them even knowing it?

I don't know about Rick, but I was afraid that whatever the malady Dr. Harvey was afflicted with might be contagious. I wanted to get out of his office as quickly as possible. We never did return to that church. But we were not going to give up that easily.

We continued going from church to church looking for someone who would respond favorably toward our beliefs. There was no variety we excluded. Based on our conversation with Dr. Harvey we developed a standard test to use in our search. First, we would tell them how God had been answering our prayers and watch their reaction. If they passed that test we would go on to tell them how the devil was after us and see how they responded to that. We would usually talk to the pastor if we could get to him. Otherwise, we would talk to someone who seemed to be an integral part of the church. We naively supposed that either the pastor or the parishioner could serve as official spokespersons not only for their local congregation but also for every congregation in every other church of that particular brand. I guess we never thought about these people being individuals with their own personal preconceived notions.

We continued for some time trying larger churches. But so few of them passed either test, and none of them passed both, that we eventually moved on to smaller congregations. On a whole, they fared better than the large churches had, but here again, none of them came out of both tests with colors flying.

We eventually came to the conclusion that the best thing we could do was stay away from churches altogether. Organized religion in general and the institutional church, in particular, held nothing of value for us it seemed. They all appeared to have what I called Churchianity, like Dr. Harvey, rather than Christianity. No matter what they called themselves they didn't take the Bible seriously. We appeared to be one step or more ahead of them already. At least we believed the Bible. We concluded that if we were blind enough to let the blind lead us then we deserved to fall into the ditch with them. So we decided to stay away from them.

As usual, however, we took things to the extreme. We didn't even want people associating us with the church world, so we stopped calling ourselves Christians, for that name, so we thought, came with a pre-packaged definition that did not describe who we were. No, the only hope was to start over again. And since we were no longer going to call ourselves Christians we were immediately faced with the problem of how to identify our belief system.

Justus wouldn't do anymore. True, God is just, but that was only one facet of our message. Warners was out because that described what we did, not who we were. Believers came close but it failed to specify what it was that we believed.

Sitting around my kitchen table pondering the question one evening, Al suddenly lit up like a light bulb,

"Istinity!" He stood to his feet with his vertical index finger raised above his head.

"What?" several of us asked at once.

"Istinity," He repeated himself, "That's what we should call ourselves."

"Why? What does that mean?" Rick wanted to know.

"It doesn't mean anything!" Al replied.

"Where did you get it?" Dave wondered.

"Nowhere."

"What do you mean nowhere?" I asked. "You say you didn't get it anywhere, and it doesn't mean anything. What kind of nonsense is this?"

"That's just it," Al responded. "I made it up. Since it doesn't exist, it doesn't have a meaning. We can use it to mean whatever we want it too."

"That's about the stupidest thing I ever heard!" Dave criticized.

"No," Rick held up his hand. "Listen! This might just be the answer we're looking for."

"I think it's ingenious," I spoke up.

"Then Istinity it is!" Al stuck his arm straight out, his hand balled into a fist.

Rick placed his hand over the top of Al's.

"I'm for it."

I did the same,

"I'm in."

"Whatever," Dave acted disgusted as he placed his hand over our three.

Al did the countdown,

"One, two three . . ." and we all shouted together as we threw our hands into the air, "Istinity!!!"

And Istinity it was. Not only for our faith, but from that time forward for our band as well.

It was after this that the lyrics of our songs became more than just apocalyptic; they took on a tone of worship as well. We tried to give God the glory for what He had done and was continuing to do for us in the words of our compositions.

And we had daily reminders of exactly what He was doing for us, for the demons were never more than just an arm's length away. If we began to deviate in the least from what little we understood of a Biblical lifestyle, the demonic activity would increase almost immediately. We had to stay on the straight and narrow way to keep them at bay.

As for Reggie, our drummer, he couldn't seem to decide if the spirits were enemies or allies. That made him a weak link in our line of defense–something we couldn't afford. We parted ways with him and soon found another drummer in the person of Bob Keller, who was of all things–a biker. He was a real work of art; truly one of a kind. Generally, he was out in la–la land somewhere, hardly aware of what was going on around him. But when something demanded his attention he would pull back into himself and tune in to earth long enough to focus on the situation at hand. Madcap is the best way to describe both his drumming technique and his personality. He was just plain off the wall.

So Istinity was now made up of four pacifists with a biker drummer: an incongruous mix if ever there was one. But Bob seemed more than willing to fraternize with us so the blend worked well. And he completely bought into our spiritual worldview. In fact those two interfaces–that we were all outcasts and that we all shared a common worldview, was what made the fit between peaceniks and biker work.

Bob lived in the woods with his elderly parents who took an intense liking to all of us. Perhaps it was because nobody had ever accepted their son so completely before. They just adopted us all and let us cohabitate with them and take over their extensive acreage. We moved our bands' equipment there and used their house as our central gathering place. It became a home to most of us.

I could never understand Bob's zany behavior. He often did things to himself that nobody in their right mind would do. At times, he would dive off the roof of their single-story house and land in a summersault on the ground. It was a feat that would kill some people and hospitalize anyone it didn't. On other occasions, he would run full force into a tree head first like a mad bull. It should have fractured his skull or broke his neck. Yet none of his antics fazed him in the least. He seemed to be indestructible–hard as a rock.

Even though I had become a pacifist I knew well that the rest of the world was not, and that made it comforting to have someone like Bob around. There were times when he turned out to be a good source of protection. It may have been hypocritical, but peace lover or not, on all such occasions my attitude was, "*Go get 'em Bob!*" And woe be to the one who brought his wrath down upon themselves.

CHAPTER 6

KILL A COMMIE FOR CHRIST

The music was good, very good, especially for a three–piece garage band. What was all the more re-markable was that their equipment was so basic. It was obvious that it took unusual musical prowess to pull off their blues–rock mix so well. The band's name was displayed on the front of the bass drum–*Antiso-cial*.

"Funny name for a group singing songs that major on the social evils of our day." I thought. I was a bit disillusioned about social issues at that moment. Hav-ing returned from the 1967 Washington D.C. march on the Pentagon only a couple of days before, I had seen enough action, both social and antisocial to last me for some time to come.

The dance seemed completely out of place in its setting. We were in the basement of a church; the local Unitarian Church. Here we were again, *'spiritual wickedness in high places'*.

During break time, Barbara, the girl who had in-vited me to this event introduced me to the front man for the group who was both singer and guitarist.

"Danny, this is Max. He's a musician too. He plays guitar."

"Oh, really," The heavy, course bearded, singers interest seemed piqued.

"And he plays in a band named–" she stopped short and turning to me asked,

"What is the name of your band, again Max?"

Taking a deep breath, I said in a sort of sigh "Istin-ity."

"Anyway, they have an emphasis too."

"And what would that be?" Danny looked at me. Before I could get it out Barbara answered.

"Oh, they're a Christian band. They play songs about spiritual issues."

Immediately something sprung up in Danny's eyes causing them to glare at me. He leaned forward and put his face uncomfortably close to mine. Then what I thought I had seen in his eyes identified itself by snarling in a whisper through his curled lip and clenched teeth,

"*Kill a Commie for Christ!*" the voice mocked in a gurgling growl from somewhere deep within Danny's throat. It didn't sound much like the Danny who had been speaking a moment before.

"What?" I was shocked. Glancing up at my friend I saw her now slowly backing away holding her hand, palm out beside her stunned and grinning face, waving bye–bye with its fingertips as she disappeared into the crowd.

Turning back to Danny I asked, "What do you mean?" more out of surprise than anything.

Danny seemed to snap back to himself, but I had to wonder where the owner of the voice had gone. Wherever it went it seemed to still be influencing what Danny now said.

"All you institutional Christians are so hypocriti-cal. Every church I know of condones the war in Viet–Nam. And you are all so bull–headed about Com-munism being the *Great Evil*! But look at the atrocities the church committed in the Crusades and Inquisi-tions!"

Momentarily forgetting the spirit, I responded to Danny instead of it,

112

"Hey Bud, you're the one who's playing in a church! What's that about? Huh?" I thrust.

"This isn't one of your everyday run–of–the–mill Christian churches," Danny parried. "Besides, even if it were, we preach our message on any platform we get a chance to."

"There you have it! You '*preach*'!" I touched.

"What's your point?" He asked.

"My point is that you assume too much. Since you're playing in a church and you preach I would assume that you were a Christian. But now it seems otherwise."

"Well I am a Christian but I'm like this Church: not one of your everyday run–of–the–mill Christians!" Danny's speech had turned staccato as he pronounced *Christians* with a hissing drawn out–S, tilting his wide–eyed head to one side. In the split–second it took to pronounce the word I distinctly saw a spirit flash in his eyes as it passed through.

I ignored it again knowing that sometimes that worked best. *Choose your battles wisely* they say.

"Point made!" I declared. "I rest my case. Don't assume that because someone calls my band Christian we are part of the institutional church."

"Well if I wasn't part of the church I wouldn't be calling myself Christian. How can you expect people to think anything different?" We were back to Danny now.

"We don't call ourselves Christians. That was our friend over there," I nodded my head toward the table where Barbara stood beside the punch bowl sipping from a cup as she conversed with several others. I explained it one more time. "That's why we made up a name for ourselves, so people wouldn't identify us with the rest of Christianity. Like I said before we call ourselves Istinity. We are Istinits."

113

"Who ever heard of such a stupid thing?" Danny ridiculed.

"Someone who names their band Antisocial and then writes songs about social issues," I rejoined.

"So?"

"It's so hypocritical," I turned his own word back on him. By now the break was over and they were calling Danny back to his microphone and guitar.

He turned and stalked away toward his drums. I had had enough for one night. I left the church and went home.

Kill a Commie for Christ? Yes, that's what he–or it said.

Great! Now the demons are going political on us! I thought.

I had already some time before, concluded that much of the war, violence, killing, and bloodshed in our world are nothing but a spillover of a battle being waged elsewhere. While I certainly did not pretend to know everything about the cloak and dagger business of dealing with the devils I was pretty sure about one thing; Communism, as well as politics in general, were the same thing as Dr. Harvey's *Churchianity*. They were all nothing but the devil's straw dummy decoys to divert our attention from the real issues; a smoke screen for the real antagonist to hide behind. *To win a war you must first properly define the enemy.*

Anyway, I knew that Christ would not have me kill anybody. Still I had to admit that untold millions have been killed in His name. It is satan[1] that would have me kill for Christ. And he would probably rather I did it in that name than any other.

---

[1] It is neither a typo nor a misprint that satan is spelled throughout this book with a small "s." It is intentional.

If Danny had known the truth, I had already had more direct contact with communism than he or most people in our culture were likely to have in a lifetime.

My first encounter with communism came when an ad appeared in the *Akron Beacon Journal* announcing a vigil for peace in Vietnam that was going to be held in downtown Akron on the corner of South Main and Mill Streets. I was interested. My feelings about the Vietnam conflict ran deep. I had already taken over a Christian Coffee House on one occasion and gave the crowd an in–your–face speech about the atrocities of the war. So, I made my way along with Rick, Al, and Dave, to the advertised gathering. Our Drummer, Bob Keller had no interest in the Vietnam conflict unless it would be for the government to revoke his mental health awarded 4–F status and send him there.

The rally consisted of a banner stretched between two hand held poles that read, "Peace in Vietnam," with about two dozen of us making our statement by standing under it. Most of us could be recognized as a part of the hippy movement. I was surprised to learn that there were so many others from the same counterculture in the Akron area yet we had known nothing about each other. This was the event that was waiting to happen that would bring us all together for the first time. What surprised me even more were the organizers of the vigil. I would have expected somebody a little more radical in appearance.

The leader was George Robinson who appeared to be in his mid–fifties and wore an orange–checkered long–sleeved flannel cowboy shirt with the arms rolled up and cowboy boots that had his jeans tucked into the top. A bush of closely cropped, curly brown hair topped his square head like an island in the sky. The most outstanding feature about this thin wrangler was his grotesquely damaged right eye that stared off in its own direction seeing nothing. What was left of the scrambled blue it had once been was covered over with a pale film.

His companion Terrance, for I discovered that they were lovers, was a good deal shorter and much thicker, sporting a short Julius Caesar haircut and wearing a burgundy pull over sweater, jeans, and sneakers. George was the older of the two by more than a decade.

For the first few minutes of the vigil people just passed by avoiding eye contact with us. Soon someone supportive enough stopped to encourage us. We asked them to join us, and they did. As people continued to stop and speak I began to appreciate the depth of political thought in the others around me. That was something I did not personally possess.

Before long I realized that many of the others attending this vigil were not people looking for a cause as my friends and I were; they were people who had, for the most part, already settled on one. And I found that to be a bit unsettling, knowing that people with an off–kilter cause can be the most difficult and dangerous to deal with.

Shortly a businessman carrying an attaché case came by and got into a heated discussion with us. While he was yet speaking a fully uniformed soldier and his friend stopped and got into an argument with the businessman, the soldier telling him that he had been to Vietnam and so, he authoritatively insisted, whatever he had to say trumped anything the businessman could say. The soldier then proceeded to tell the businessman and the others who by now had stopped to listen, that he had fought for the freedom of our country and that included the likes of us having the right to express our opinion about the war he fought in. Boy, you talk about war making for strange bed partners.

Then George, addressing the private, stepped into the conversation.

"How can you possibly call fighting a bunch of North Vietnam farmers, defending our freedom?" He asked.

The businessman answered for the private. "Well anyone with any sense knows that if we don't fight them over there we will have to fight them here."

"And how are they going to get here?" George asked, "In row boats?" He grinned as he gave a knowing look around the chuckling crowd.

Now the private took up the debate.

"For one thing mister we are not fighting North Vietnam farmers. They are a highly developed and deadly army. For that matter we are fighting more than the North Vietnam army. We are fighting Communism in general."

"And what if they did bring their communism here? Pure Marxism isn't a bad thing you know," George stared defiantly.

Long story made short, it got ugly. I mean the soldier grabbed the cowboy and shook him up kind of ugly.

Then the businessman and several others grabbed the soldier and restrained him lest he get himself arrested. George continued his taunting as the soldier quit the field rather than twist the philosophizing Marxist into a pretzel.

The soldier and his friend walked down the street with him shouting over his shoulder,

"You aren't worth the effort it would take to whip you! Good thing you've got some sympathizers besides me to help protect you man! You are an idiot!"

Now the businessman turned his guns on George again,

"And don't you think for a minute that I'm one of those sympathizers! I just didn't want a man who put his life on the line for our freedom to end up in jail over the likes of you."

He stormed off in the same direction the soldier had gone with George hurling his sardonic words down the street after him.

This guy is an idiot, I thought to myself. *It's a wonder that he hasn't had more than his eye rear-ranged."*

About an hour later as the vigil came to an end George asked my friends and I where we lived. As it turned out he and Terrance had recently moved into a large house about a block west of mine on the same street. We had seen cars around the place with bumper stickers protesting the war in Vietnam and wondered who had moved in. George and Terrance offered us a ride home. After rolling up the banner, and fastening it to the side of the car we all piled in.

Upon arriving at George and Terrance's place they invited us in for coffee. We accepted and there met two more of their *comrades*. One was forty–some year-old Margaret who spoke little, and when she did her cleft palate told the story behind her silence. She wore her short black hair very conventionally and was dressed in a sheer white blouse with a gray wool skirt. I would have thought her to be a middle–class working mother from the fifties. Her tall, slender companion was the articulate black haired Ron who wore a white shirt, and dress pants.

The house was finely furnished, the most out-standing feature being the conservatory. There sat a baby grand piano, a set of drums, an upright bass, a trombone and a harp. We told them that we were members of a band ourselves.

George said,

"I love music more than most. Jazz is my forte. But music should never be an end in itself. It can be such a powerful vehicle to get a message across."

We sat on the overstuffed furniture in the living room while Margaret went to fix the coffee. The conversation seemed to flit aimlessly from subject to subject as we each picked the others brains in an effort to assess one another.

The conversation began to take form when George eventually warmed up to the idea of us getting together regularly every week to discuss politics, religion, economics and whatever else might come up. He suggested Wednesday evenings, the next of which was only two days away. Once we had agreed they encouraged us to bring our friends.

We concluded the evening by gathering around the piano with Margaret playing what George would call, *a song with a message*: "*We Shall Overcome*."

On our way to my house Dave was the first to speak.

"I don't know about these guys. I don't like the vibes I'm getting."

"What do you mean?" Rick asked.

"Well I was kind of scared. Like there was something more underneath everything they were saying."

"Like what?" asked Al.

Dave got defensive, "I don't know–Ok?! For one thing, I've always heard that *We Shall Overcome* is a communist song!"

"Come on man! Don't be so leery. They're ok. Wouldn't you say so Max?" Al glanced at me. For once I found myself agreeing with Dave. That was rare.

"Well I don't know. I'm a little skeptical myself. I felt something sinister there."

"I think they're communist!" Dave came out with it. "You know what they call these little groups of commies that get together don't you? They call them a cell group. Guys, we just set up a meeting with a communist cell group!"

"Naw!" Al shook his head.

"Listen guys, by what I hear communists can be as bad as the Mafia." Dave warned.

I wasn't quite ready to go that far but it was Rick who spoke up,

"One thing's for sure. Time will tell."

We never did get anybody outside of our own immediate group to the Wednesday night meetings. Just the same we continued getting together with them, and before long George and his group's socialistic tendencies began to evidence themselves in the discussions. It appeared that David's suspicions were well founded. But by now I had gotten used to the idea of them being communists. As such, they didn't seem to be a threat of any sort.

Dave was increasingly troubled about the meetings and in time refused to go any more. George took note and asked about it. Rick broke the news,

"He thinks you guys are communists. He's scared of you."

Immediately George threw up his hands and acted as if he thought it to be absolutely incredulous that anybody would think such a thing. He almost acted as if he himself thought communists to be, well—*revolting*. His comrades all agreed emphatically with him. He explained that they were Marxists, not communists going to great lengths to describe the difference. Marxism, he declared, was pure communism, a philosophy, and today's communism was a political distortion of it—not the same thing at all.

"Besides, a communist here in America would be someone who belongs to *The American Communist Party,* and has been issued an official card." Ron explained, insisting that they were not card–carrying communist.

It made no difference to me whether they were communists or not. Eventually it became clear that if they weren't, they at least had close ties and worked in tandem with the American Communist Party.

In several of our Wednesday night meetings they played recordings of folk and rock music and de-coded the lyrics for us. Now here was a twist, adults explaining to teens what their music means. When the songs were interpreted, the message was clear; com-munism–or was it Marxism? So this is what George meant when he talked about using music to get a mes-sage across.

In other meetings, they supplied us with com-munist literature such as *The Daily Worker* newspa-per and eventually got around to giving us copies of the American Communists Party's Constitution. All this was, of course, *just for discussion purposes*. Hold the phone! Where did these Marxists get all that Com-munist stuff?

The Marxists (I guess) later offered us the oppor-tunity to move into an upstairs apartment in their house–no charge. Rick and Dave took them up on it. As if that weren't enough, they fed us at times as well. It only served to make me wonder all the more why they were investing so much in us. What were they af-ter?

We became curious as to how these people were fi-nanced. None of them worked a regular job. These rep-resentatives of the workingman weren't workingmen themselves. They appeared to be devoted to spreading their Marxist doctrine full–time. Yet for all that, they lived pretty luxuriously. We finally just asked them. The answer surprised us.

"Well, we own a recording studio in Maryland that someone runs for us and we live off the profits."

That was the wrong thing to say to a group of as-piring musicians who felt they had a similar message to share. It seemed logical that these were precisely the people who should help us cut a record, you know, just for the sake of the cause. We were sure that it was exactly what we needed to jump–start our music career. This was a Godsend!

They seemed indifferent when we made the suggestion to them. In spite of repeated attempts, we never saw the inside of their studio–if there was one.

The more involved we became with this group the more gaping the discrepancies we saw in their story line. Many of these contradictions were so blatant that I personally considered them an insult to my intelligence; as if I was so dumb as to not notice the inconsistencies in these lame attempts at deception.

We soon realized that we couldn't believe anything any of them said, especially George. We had caught him in more lies than either he or we could keep track of. Either he wasn't good at them or he was just too prolific to keep them all in order. You've heard of the breed before – *pathological liars*. In George's case, it was so extreme that it smacked of someone being compelled by an outside force; and there certainly was that aura about George; that strange presence that he ever bore. You could always sense that it was there working just out of sight. Maybe that was why he didn't care whether his lies fit together or not, so long as they had the immediate effect he was after.

Besides they did teach that *the end justifies the means*, and they were consistent enough to live like they believed it.

Why would anyone bother teaching such a thing? I wondered. *It's inconsistent and self–defeating. If such a teaching were true who would believe the teachings of the teacher? Might not such a teacher have the end of deceiving his or her students in view by the means of the teaching?*

It only served to fuel my skepticism. What were these guys up too?

Come October these acquaintances of ours provided us with a ride to Washington D.C. for the first major Anti–Vietnam demonstration there. We started at the Lincoln Memorial a hundred thousand strong, all gathered around the reflection pool listening to folk singer *Phil Ochs*. Then at least thirty-five thousand of us led by Revolutionary celebrity Abbie Hoffman marched across the Arlington Memorial Bridge and down the Jefferson Davis Highway to the Pentagon on the Virginia side of the Potomac River where we were greeted in its 67–acre parking lot by 2,500 armed soldiers and a host of U.S. Marshalls. They had erected a fence across the front of the building to keep us at a safe distance but the sheer number of protestors toppled sections of it.

I watched as one heavy boy clambered over the fence and plopped his 300–pound plus body on the ground. It took four soldiers to carry his dead weight out of there. As soon as they dumped him on the other side of the fence he jumped up, ran back to the fence, quickly climbed over and again dropped to the ground on the other side. After several repeats of the same antic the soldiers took him to a paddy wagon and hauled him off to jail. He was one of about seven hundred arrested before it was over.

There was a plot afoot to display the reality of *flower power* by airdropping 10,000 blossoms on the Pentagon. Alas an undercover agent discovered and foiled the plan. So the flowers were handed out to everyone instead. Many of them found their way to the front lines where soldier and protestor stood toe–to–toe, and there they were placed into the barrels of the soldiers' guns.

The demonstration was peaceful enough until the civil disobedience on the front steps of the Pentagon erupted into violence. That was the point at which I decided the whole business was getting too serious for me and left. Having become separated from Al, Dave, Rick and our ride, I roamed the streets of Washington alone looking for them.

As the night wore on I passed thousands of demonstrators all over the city sleeping in tents or under the open sky; some sitting around campfires, drinking liquor and taking drugs. This was my first contact with the developing hippie movement at large. I was amazed that rather than feeling a kindred spirit, I felt enmity emanating from these "peaceniks" toward me as I wandered aimlessly up and down the streets. 'Safe' is not the word I would use to describe the feelings I experienced that night. There seemed to be a common paranoia that anybody outside of a person's immediate group might be a narcotics agent an FBI or CIA operative or some other possible infiltrator. Suspicion was rampant. I even saw the demon glare in at least one man's eyes. The greatest fear I faced that evening was getting mugged by my own kind. Now that I think of it, I guess I was as caught up in the paranoia and suspicion as anyone.

Back at the Pentagon the vigil lasted all that night. Abbie Huffman and Jerry Rubin declared that they were going to levitate the building 300 feet into the air by means of transcendental meditation and exorcize the demons in it by shaking them out. Many who were there, swear to this day that they were momentarily successful, but I remain a solid skeptic.

That was the first time I remember thinking about the occult and communism sharing the same spiritual dimension.

Later that night George Robinson having rounded up all the others found me by the Jefferson Memorial. The protest ran on for two more days but we headed for the sweet hills of Ohio in George's station wagon. It was just after our return that I ran into Danny and his group–*Antisocial*.

Though we had become disillusioned with the church, Rick and I were still running trial and error experiments on principles we found in the Bible, and were rapidly rising to the conviction that the Bible was the only reliable source of information. Our studies in turn were forming our philosophy on affairs of state.

One of the discoveries our research turned up was that in the same place the Bible talked about *"spiritual wickedness in high places"* it also made mention of territorial spirits; entities called *"principalities"*–like municipalities, only a princedom: a geographical territory ruled by a prince–apparently a spiritual one. The Bible identified one as *"The Prince of Persia."* That sure sounded political to me.

And maybe the philosophy of Marxism was one of the many errors promoted by the *"rulers of the darkness of this world"* that were also mentioned in that same passage. Their forte seemed to be battling the light of truth by promoting the darkness of false teachings.

Then there was the teaching in another scripture about these spirit beings using what the Bible termed *imaginations* to combat truth. *Imaginations* turned out to mean *"false philosophical concepts or world views"*–like Marxism for example. In fact, the Bible itself referred to such teachings as *"doctrines of devils."* These, we concluded are used by the spirits to engender chaos around the world. I began to realize that bedlam and confusion was the name of satan's game. So that was why I couldn't make out some of the communists' logic; they were coming at the same subject as we were but from a different world view and with a hidden agenda, which they kept hidden by throwing up a smoke screen to cloak the truth. The Bible referred to such teachings as *"satanic strongholds."*

I finally told George and company that I could never be a communist because I had converted from atheism to Christianity. They laughed as George explained,

"Communism and atheism are two different things. I mean Jesus was the first communist of them all! He taught us to share what we have. The disciples and He lived a communal lifestyle."

"Ok," I said, "But for them it was voluntary, not a decision forced on them by a totalitarian government."

Ron spoke up, "Well the government control is just a stage we have to go through until everybody learns to share; until it becomes the natural thing to do. Then the government's control can be done away with."

"So what's going to purge the greed out of peoples' hearts?" I asked.

Fast as quicksilver, George responded, "Evolutionary process!"

I was dumbfounded.

"You actually think that the passing of time is going to turn humans into a benevolent and charitable race of beings?"

"That's what we believe," He stared blankly.

"Then you have more faith than I do. It's just in the wrong thing."

That's when it hit me.

"Wait a minute! Are you telling me that communism is evolution applied to politics?"

"Oh, absolutely!" George was definite.

I jumped to my feet and strode back and forth. "But there is always going to be someone who will want to sit on top of the monkey–pile, you know–want to be top dog; king of the mountain."

George shrugged with a scowl on his face.

"You're not giving the system a chance to prove itself Max."

126

I stopped and looked into George's face. "Do your leaders in Russia live on the same level as the common worker?" I asked, hinting that they themselves were not workers yet lived luxuriously.

"Everything in Russia isn't all that it should be. We've told you that before. I mean, are all the churches everything they should be?"

George was good at avoiding questions.

"So? Communism, Capitalism, Church–none of it is going to work until people start including God. And any of it might work if they did." I sat back down.

"Look," George pointed at me, "Capitalism will never work. It is the poor being slaves to the rich."

"Well it looks to me like Communism is everybody, rich and poor alike, being slaves to a handful of political gangsters," I responded, then was shocked at what had come out of my own mouth.

"Have a little faith boy!" He held his hands out.

"I do have faith, but not in politics. Man's problem is spiritual not political. He needs a spiritual cure."

"We are talking in circles here." I could tell that George was exasperated. But I went on,

"Jesus said there would be wars and rumors of wars until He returned. That tells me that He, not politics is the answer to the world's basic problems," I said flatly.

"So, I suppose you think you're going to convert the whole world!" He mocked, jumping to his feet and throwing his body back with his arms spread wide.

I threw it back at him. "Why not? You do."

"Yes, but religion won't work. Religion is the opiate of the people," George quoted Karl Marx.

"I said that the answer to man's problems was spiritual–not religious; there is a big difference," I noted. "As I see it communism itself is nothing but another form of religion."

That gave George the chance to renew his effort to convince me.

"Just my point! Look at the book of Acts. They followed Jesus' example and had all things in common."

"The only reason Bible communism, if you want to call it that, worked at all was because it was built on faith in God. Besides what happened there was only meant to be a temporary fix for a specific problem." I explained.

George rolled his good eye, "I'm telling you that you don't have to be an atheist to be a communist. They are two different things"

"Do you believe in God?" I pointed at him.

"That's beside the point," he avoided yet another question.

How about you Ron or you Margaret? What about you Terrence?" I went around the room receiving a negative reply from each one.

"Does Russia's Communist State believe in God?" I persisted.

"Like I said before, we aren't promoting Russia." He sidestepped the issue once more.

"And what about the American Communist Party? Do they believe in God?" I forced the point.

George played dumb, "What are you trying to get at?"

"You say I don't have to be an atheist to be a communist, yet everybody associated with communism is one!"

"And this is exactly why Marx said that religion is the opiate of the people." George slowly and sadly shook his head, "It kills motivation to take the right action to fix mankind's problems."

"Well I may not convert the world but at least I have to offer them what I believe will work." I said.

"Just keep an open mind and don't make too rash a decision," George suggested; it sounded like a warning.

"I won't George," I committed myself; "But I can't help being skeptical."

"Why!" George was nearly angry now.

"Because, wherever Communism takes over a purge of everyone who doesn't agree with it begins. They have never been willing to work hand in hand with the church. I heard what your leader Gus Hall said about not being satisfied until he saw the last priest strangled with the guts of the last preacher! You know heads will roll."

"Do you really think I would be a part of something like that, Max?" He asked sympathetically.

"Well, now that you put a face on it, I would have to say no," I lied.

I did think he might in fact be a part of something like that but I wasn't about to tell him. If his cause was successful, and judging from the numbers I saw in Washington I thought it well might be, I didn't want to get my name on some hit list. George's spirit always bore an element of treachery, and if the end justifies the means how could I ever trust them? Even though I wouldn't kill a Commie for Christ might not a Commie kill a Christian for the Cause? Especially if this was actually spiritual warfare coming over into the physical world, as I suspected

"By the way," I addressed George, "What about you, if the Party does take over?"

"Oh, they'll have a place for me. In fact, I would be rewarded for my faithfulness. So would you if you joined us," George offered again.

"I wouldn't trust it George. Think about it. You've been programmed to revolt against the system. If they become the system you might be the first to go. It's the only way they could be sure you won't revolt against them," I warned.

"I think we should just both try to improve the world and maybe somewhere between the two it will happen," George had given up for now. "In time you will see that American Communism is congenial."

In time what I saw was just the opposite. American Communism was not congenial. Despite my commitment, which was half–hearted and completely self–serving, from that night forward I began disassociating myself with George and his friends. Dave was relieved, neither Al nor Bob seemed to care, and Rick agreed with me.

We paid them one more visit at their request. George told us that they had to leave town but wondered if we would be interested in helping carry on the work they had begun. They especially mentioned the connections they had with the Students for a Democratic Society at Kent State University. When we hesitated, the pressure increased, again with overtones of warning.

"You need to get off the fence! Either get in or get out!" George demanded.

We left that night on an *I'll–call–you–about–it–later* basis, but I had no intentions of ever calling them again. I was doing just what George said–getting off the fence and getting out. Shortly afterwards the whole group dropped out of sight. I never saw or heard of any of them again. While my friends and I did nothing more to further their cause others did pick up where they left off, among them a few of our acquaintances.

The following year I received a summons in the mail from my neighbors and our government to appear at the local Greyhound bus station for a ride to Cleveland where I would be given a free physical exam to see if I was suitable material for the military. I boarded the specially chartered bus carrying a 2-inch-thick 18 by 12 inch commentary on the Gospel of Matthew under my arm just in case I had a chance to do a little reading. We were no sooner rolling down the road than the fellow sitting beside me spoke.

"Can you believe this garbage?"

"What's that?" I looked up from my reading.

"This whole draft thing," He waved his hand in the air. He went on to state how corrupt the government was and how immoral the war in Vietnam was. Next thing I knew he wasn't sitting beside me anymore. Instead he was up front standing beside the bus driver and telling the whole bus that they didn't have to put up with this nonsense. They didn't have to go into the armed forces or go to Vietnam. They could refuse. Then this evangel of politics used the same familiar argument I had heard before—I knew it had to come from the same source, for even the phraseology and tonal inflections were the same.

"They say we have to fight them there or we will end up fighting them here. How can a bunch of North Vietnam farmers get over here to fight us? In row boats?"

He's not one of us. How did he get on here without the letter? I wondered. I had to show mine. *And why doesn't that bus driver stop him right now?*

Then I realized that they were in cahoots. I couldn't believe it. Either somebody had paid the bus driver off or, and this was more likely, some communist had gotten a job in the Greyhound Bus Line and manipulated themselves into the position of driving selective service draftees to Cleveland so they could let propagandists on board to preach their doctrine.

After passing out some papers my friend sat down next to me again. We rode the rest of the way to Cleveland in silence. When we arrived as we were exiting the bus it was obvious that the *comrade* wasn't going with us. I started down the aisle then paused momentarily turned, looked at my traveling companion and said,

"Now you be sure to give my regards to George Robinson. You hear?"

He was shocked and started to ask,

"How did . . . " But I was gone.

Inside the building, I fell in line. The fellow behind me asked about the book I was carrying.

"It's a commentary about the Bible," I showed it to him.

"Oh! So, you're a Christian huh?"

"Yes, I guess you could call me that," I shook my head, tired of explaining the Istinity thing.

"I want to debate you," He challenged.

"What are you talking about?"

"I'm a Black Muslim, I want to debate you," He demanded.

"I'm not debating anyone."

"You're afraid!"

"Of what?"

"To debate me."

"What's there to debate?"

"Whose religion is the best."

"I'm not looking for religion," I gazed into his hollow eyes "I'm just trying to find peace and truth. You got a corner on that?"

"Come on! I challenge you! Debate with me."

I refused to say another word. Standing in my silence I thought to myself,

What is this? If it's not the Communists it's the Muslims, if it's not the Muslims it's the Church, if it's not the Church it's the demons, and if it's not any of them it's the government.

We were conducted to an elevator that took us to the 25th floor of the building. There they had us disrobe and twist into all sort of undignified positions so they could examine . . . well, us. At one point the man up front asked if anyone had any rashes. I raised my hand. He walked over and asked where the rash was. I told him it was behind my ear. He took a quick look then pulled me out of line,

"Go sit over there." He pointed at a row of chairs.

Soon a uniformed man came to get me. I followed him into his coldly decorated office. While he filled out papers I stood at the ceiling to floor window that looked to the east over downtown Cleveland and Lake Erie. I felt strange standing there more undressed than not. Finally, the doctor, for so the name plate on his desk called him, grabbed a large rubber stamp and pounded it down on the paperwork.

"Go put your clothes on," he held the papers out for me to take.

I was confused.

"Should I . . ."

"I SAID GO PUT YOUR CLOTHES ON!!" he screamed.

I nearly jumped out of my skin; after all it was about all I had on.

"Yes Sir!" I scampered out of his office.

After getting dressed, as I was being ushered to another department in the basement of the same building my escort and I stood waiting for the elevator. The rest of my previous group came walking by in nothing but their skivvies. I spied my Muslim agitator among them. He stopped as they passed by,

"What's up here? Why are you dressed? Did they reject you?"

"I'm not sure," I told him.

"They did!" he confidently replied. "You wouldn't be dressed already if they hadn't."

My uniformed escort broke in.

"He's right. You wouldn't be going where I'm taking you if they hadn't."

"Oh," I raised my eyebrows.

"You know why they rejected you don't you?" the debater asked.

"Uh, no–do you?" I wondered.

"It's because you carry that big black book," He pointed at the commentary under my arm as if I had purposely portrayed lunacy.

I looked at him narrowly, leaned close and whispered in his ear,

"Why do you think I carry this big black book?"

He looked at me in silence.

"Jealous?" I asked. He responded,

"OOOOOOO!" and he marched off down the hall after the rest of the group.

In the basement an attractive young nurse about my own age interviewed me.

"Do you know why you are here?"

"No," I played dumb.

"It's because they are not accepting you into the armed forces," She verified.

Silence.

"Do you have any idea why?" she tilted her pretty head.

"Because I have a rash behind my ear?" I asked.

"No, try again." She said.

"Really, I don't have a clue. They asked if anyone had a rash, I told them I did, they sent me off with some doctor and here I am."

"Come on now, guess one more time–just for me." She suggested looking at me as sympathetically as she might a puppy.

"Well," I ventured, "Does it have anything to do with being emotionally disturbed?"

"Ah–ha, now we're getting somewhere," she declared smiling at me.

"Some of my friends have used the word 'schizophrenic' to describe me," I admitted.

"Bingo!" She rejoined "And the last thing you need is the army."

"I supposed the last thing the army needs is me," I turned the statement on its head.

"Likely," She agreed. "But what you do need is a good psychiatrist. So I'll set you up with an appointment."

After some arranging she gave me a piece of paper with a name, address, and date for follow–up.

A professional friend of mine later told me in all sincerity,

"Max–don't go to that appointment. I'm telling you if you do they'll never let you go. They'll lock you up."

I was amazed. I didn't think I was all that bad or that schizophrenia was contagious. But he scared me enough that I thought I'd better not take the chance.

Since I didn't keep my appointment they sent a psychiatric nurse to visit me at our house. I told her in no uncertain terms that I didn't want their kind of help. So one trip finished her. I never heard from them again. I suppose they had enough sense to know that you can't help someone who doesn't want help.

So, I was officially classified as 4–F which I guess meant they didn't ever want to see me again under any circumstances.

May 5, 1970

The radio announced that smoke was rising from the burned out remains of the ROTC building at Kent State University. Protestors had set the fire and the National Guard had shot four students to death and wounded nine others. It had the surrealism of a night-mare about it.

I visited my old friend Dale Cardigan shortly there-after. He was the main figure George Robinson's group secured to take over their activities. A member of the Students for a Democratic Society, Dale was ever po-litically minded. In fact, he did a stint in jail when he flipped out over a George Wallace bumper sticker dur-ing the 1968 presidential race and broke every window out of the car. Dale's political activism culminated in the history–changing Kent State shootings that stopped Americas radical revolutionary movement dead in its tracks.

My visit to Dale was to get the inside story. Every-body around him was wearing black rags tied around their left arm in memory of the *Kent State Four*. They were all cursing the system and saying that it was time to change their methods.

"We need to cut our hair, put on three piece suits and infiltrate the system," Dale told me.

During our conversation, I learned that the Amer-ican Communist Party, compliments of George Robin-son, supplied Dale and the other organizers of the May 1–4 protest with busloads of outsiders to beef up the violence. Both the organizers and the bused in com-munists had used anyone they could to generate strife including the great number of bikers who were pre-sent, drawn by nothing other than the attraction of an-archy. In fact, they were the ones who sparked the whole thing off.

It was then that I was sure that our bass player Dave had been right all along. We had been consorting with a cell group of professional communist agitators, financed by the American Communist Party. This was the grand finale of the work that they had started with groups like the one my friends and I had been part of.

I also realized that the conflict with the devil and his forces that my friends and I had been fighting was just one battle in a much greater war that was being played out on a world–wide scale. satan, cannot rest content to control only the lives of individuals. He wants to control the masses as well. Spiritual warfare is no game. It is serious business and the stakes are high. The devil wants to control the whole world and George's subtle threats let me know that getting in the devil's way by speaking the truth can be perilous. There are times when people die for telling the truth.

CHAPTER 7

DRUGS

A single naked light bulb, hanging from the ceiling by its cord, provided the only light for the room. Upon entry, the visitor was greeted by deep chestnut walls, every inch covered with white graffiti, most of it religious in nature. The pictures and text were scrawled so tightly together that they occasionally overlapped. The wall script told its own story; the occupant of this room was searching for something spiritual in nature. Some of the sayings were from the Bible and some from eastern religions: Buddhism and Hinduism, while others appeared to be from the Catholic Church. There were also ventings of frustration and anger along with questions about the meaning of life events complete with possible answers. The one thing noticeably missing from the crude mural was sex; not a word or picture about it. This wall scrawl appeared to be an unconventional diary. Above the head of the big brass bed with its' soiled mattress was drawn an enormous multi–colored cross with light rays shooting out from it in every direction and a crown hovering above it. A single, large, bold, word capped the crucifix's scene: INSTINITY. Though we never knew it, Dino had been a follower of our band and its religious overtones for some time. He had become obsessed with our message which he had unfortunately only gotten part of. The only other thing in the room was a small desk pushed closely into the corner accompanied by a wobbly wooden captain's chair with a conspicuously missing left arm. Oh yes, there was one more element: blood. It covered the floor at the entrance of the room, just to the left of the bed, and the back bottom third of the door, splattering outward in every direction covering the dark walls with a lighter red, and speckling the white ceiling. It was the blood of a young coed from the University of Akron who had come to this room in the cheap dollar-a-night hotel on the east side of town looking for something to liven up the party she was about to attend. She came but she never left; at least not alive. Nor had she come alone. Two male friends, one of them her finance, had accompanied her–just in case.

Having made their way down the dimly lit hallway on the third floor they knocked at the door of room 307, which opened only as far as the safety chain would allow. An eye peering out though the crack asked gruffly

"What do you want?"

"We heard that we could get some smokes here," came the answer.

"What kind?" the eye asked.

"Special blends of Persian tobacco" one of the three students answered, repeating the code they had been told to use.

That answer gave Dino the all clear signal, whereupon the door was flung open wide and the three invited in.

Dino stood there in his bare feet with no shirt and totally unkempt black hair that hung to his shoulders. Closing the door behind them he said to the boys,

"Have a seat," motioning for them to use the edge of the bed.

"And a chair for the young lady," He said picking up the old wooden seat at the desk and placing it directly behind her. Then stepping back he asked,

"What did you have in mind?" looking from one student to another.

"Well we're going to a party tonight," the girl began to explain but was interrupted by one of the boys,

"And we just wanted to liven things up a bit. A little marijuana was all we had in mind," he said.

"How much?"

"A nickel bag" the other boy answered using the slang that he had learned meant five dollars' worth.

"Done!" said Dino. Reaching into a drawer of the desk behind him he pulled out a plastic baggy which he held up in front of his face.

"Ta–ta!"

The girl fished deep into her satchel producing a crumpled five–dollar bill which she handed to Dino in exchange for the plastic baggie. This she buried deep in the bottom of her bag.

They sat for some time quizzing Dino about the drug scene. This was the first time any of the three had ever been in direct contact with anyone from it. Dino was in his glory. He loved being the expert for a change. The trio began to relax, surprised by this animated, witty, charismatic young man. He was not at all what they had anticipated. Even his appearance was inconsistent with the charming lad before them. They thought themselves foolish to have been so anxious about coming. What they didn't know was that the Dino they were communicating with was the by–product of the acid (LSD) trip he was on.

One of the boys pulled a pack of cigarettes out of his shirt pocket and asked Dino if he minded.

"Naw–go ahead," he said.

Discovering that the pack was empty the young man swore.

"Hey, no problem man. They got a machine down in the lobby," Dino said.

"Oh yeah, I saw it as we came up now that you mention it."

The boy stood to his feet and announced that he would be right back.

"Hold up man!" the other said as he jumped up. "I'll go with you. I've got to use the bathroom."

"We'll be right back Susan" the boy said looking at his fiancé.

"We'll be fine," Dino answered for her, to which she shook her head affirmatively.

Once they were gone and the door closed Dino asked,

"So, it's Susan, is it?"

"Yes"

"Do they call you Susan, or do you prefer Susie or just Sue?" He inquired.

"It really doesn't matter to me."

Susan continued to carry on the conversation where her two friends had left off. Being the most inquisitive of the three she had been carrying the bulk of it anyway. She was fascinated by the prospect of altered states of mind through the use of chemicals.

The talk drifted from drug type to drug type: the varieties of hallucinogens, then uppers, and downers followed by the opiates. After the discussion moved on to methods of use, they soon came to the subject of needles. That was when the conversation really sparked. To Susan intravenous injection was the big bad boy of the drug scene and she found its forbidden stigma enticing. Dino picked up on it and asked,

"Have you ever seen anybody shoot up?"

"No, I can't say that I have."

"Would you like to?"

"What? Right here and now?"

"Sure—why not?"

"Well I wouldn't want you to do it just for me—but if you were going to anyway . . ."

"I shoot what they call speed; crystal meth."

Susan had heard of it. In fact, she had a button back in her dorm room that someone had given her that warned, "SPEED KILLS!" She was about to find out that it did it in more ways than one.

"OK!" she said with anticipation.

Dino opened the bottom drawer of the desk and pulled out the necessary paraphernalia. There was a long piece of surgical rubber tubing, a bottle cap, an eyedropper and a syringe. He then opened the middle drawer of the desk and brought out a pack of white substance.

"I'll need to use the chair." He said, "You can sit over here on the edge of the bed."

They traded places. Sitting in the chair Dino began his ritualistic preparation explaining every step along the way to Susan.

"First you put some of the meth into the cap." He unwrapped the package and tapped a small amount of the substance into it.

"Then you mix it with water," he stuck the eye dropper into a glass sitting on the desk and added some to the bottle cap.

"Don't you have to measure that stuff?" Susan wondered.

"Not when you've been doing it as long as I have. You get to knowing how much to use" Dino explained.

"Now you take the needle . . ."

"I thought you had to heat it," Susan interjected.

"No that's smack . . . heroin. You have to heat that because it doesn't mix with water as easy as meth." He continued

"Now you draw the solution up into the needle." He did so.

"What does it feel like? You know—the drug?"

Dino glanced up "Like Nirvana baby!"

He wrapped the surgical hose around his bicep and tightened it holding the rubber between his clenched teeth. Forming a fist the blood vessels in his forearm began to stand out. He said, as clearly as he could with his teeth clamped down on the tubing,

"Now you stick the needle into your arm." He pushed the point through his skin.

"I always pull it out a little first to make sure I hit the vein," he said. When he did blood mingled with the liquid in the syringe.

"Then you push the syringe down."

Dino didn't notice but as he was shooting the crystal meth into his arm he began chewing his lip where it was holding the rubber hose. A stream of blood began to flow freely from it as he released the tubing. Susan, who had by now stood up from the bed and moved closer placing her face near the injection site for a better view, looked up and saw the gushing blood. Startled she jumped back and screamed.

What happened next nobody can fully explain. Likely it was part of the psychosis speed tends to create mixed with hallucination from the LSD. By Dino's own account he didn't see Susan, but a horrific and twisted demonic assailant instead. He jumped to his feet, the needle still hanging from his arm and knocked Susan to the floor. Grabbing the captain's chair, he swung it in a wide arch over his head bringing it down in a crushing blow upon Susan's skull, breaking the chair into a dozen pieces. Knocked senseless, with blood streaking her blonde hair, Susan tried to stand but fell against the door. Dino grabbed the broken off arm of the chair and began screaming about Susan being the devil and attacked, pummeling her violently with his makeshift club. And with that he made the final entry into his diary on the wall; this one written in red.

The two men on their way back from the lobby heard a dull methodical pounding the moment they stepped off the elevator at the third floor. They thought little of it at first, but the nearer they drew to room 307 the louder it became. Looking at one another they sprinted for the room. Upon arriving they knew for certain that the sound was coming from inside. They tried the door but the weight of Susan's body lying against it made it impossible to open completely. Through the crack one of the boys saw a hand swinging a wooden chair arm slinging blood in all directions.

He screamed and renewed his effort at opening the door. Both he and his friend ran against it with their shoulders. The door breaking from its hinges gave way. There stood Dino, wild eyed and covered with Susan's blood. Her body lay on the floor, its head an unrecognizable mass of blood, bone, and tissue.

Dino quickly and quietly submitted to the boys burying his face into his hands. The police were called with whom Dino went willingly. The traumatic shock of the experience sent Susan's fiancé to a psychiatric ward for an extended stay; Dino was prosecuted to the fullest extent of the law by the state of Ohio; and Susan became the latest victim of the vice demon that receives its delegated authority from the principality under which it operates. It seems that there was more truth in what one meth–head told me than I realized at the time: "crystal meth is the devil's serum! It comes straight out of hell!" he declared. These vice spirits, designated in the scriptures by the word *powers* is always concocting new ways to sin and create misery that was heretofore unknown by man.

Living in several hippie communes in the 1960's put me smack in the middle of the drug scene. I had such an intense interest in altered states of consciousness when I was younger that I tried anything I could get my hands on. But my involvement in the occult left me with the firm conviction that drug use threw my mind open to the demonic hounds of hell and I already had enough trouble from them without sending up flares telling them to come and get me. Still at times my lower nature would get the better of me and I would give in and use something, but always with a bad backlash. It was as if God had a hedge around me that kept me from delving in deeply. I knew that while others might get away with it I could never safely surrender my will to the devils. And of course stories like Dino's served only to strengthen my conviction.

And Dino's wasn't the only story I knew. There was my friend Beverly who having not shown up for several days was found on her apartment floor lying in a pool of dried up blood. She had gnawed her tongue in two and bled to death during a drug–induced seizure. She was so decomposed that they couldn't open the casket at her funeral.

Then there was another of my personal friends, the beautiful and refined preacher's daughter Linda who played a mean piano and sang like an angel. She talked to everyone about Jesus being what they were looking for but then fell into the rock scene and started using drugs heavily herself. While still in her mid–twenties, on a cold stormy night while crossing a bridge in the pouring rain she slumped to the sidewalk and left this world from an overdose.

One major issue is that a user cannot be sure about the purity of what he or she gets on the street. Sellers will sometimes put anything into their pills and powders to stretch it further or to get more kick out of it.

A perfect case in point was my friend Jack. He guarded prostitutes for their pimps in the red–light district of town and was paid for his services in heroin. But on one occasion someone had cut the heroin with the powder from fluorescent tubes, which landed him in the hospital, his arms and legs swollen pitifully. The doctor noticing needle tracks on Jack's neck told him that if he would have injected into one of those arteries, which he usually did, it would have been instant death. Jack swore that he was done using forever, even committing to pursue a college degree, but upon release from the hospital he was soon back to shooting up again. Then came the night when being penniless and needing his fix, Jack broke into an apartment to steal whatever he could to hock. The victim, an old man, woke and tried to stop him and in the ensuing struggle Jack pushed him and he fell backwards, hit his head on a piece of furniture and died. Jack spent years in the penitentiary paying for the crime.

Another example was the time that a warning was circulating to watch out for the pink pills that had been floating around. The notorious biker gang known as the *Misfits* had a "lab" in the Kenmore area of town where they made the bootlegged pink pills referred to. When the narcotics agents raided the place they discovered just how loosely the word "lab" could be used. It was a one-car garage with a dirt floor where they mixed up their basic paste in an old paint bucket on the workbench, after which they added their "secret ingredients" to the goo, one of which was rat poison which they had discovered contains strychnine which in smaller quantities creates a euphoria. They had drilled holes in some thin boards and when their pink colored gunk was smeared over them it was pressed into the openings. After the muck dried they flexed the boards and *wallah*, out popped instant pills. The side effects of such drugs were impossible to predict.

The founder of one commune I lived in for a while believed that drug use enhanced his spiritual experiences and accelerated his self–improvement. In fact he had founded the communion particularly for those on a spiritual quest. He described how on one of his LSD trips he "got all the barriers down."

"It was like unpeeling a banana one strip at a time," he said, but then lamented, "but once the drug wore off and I had to start interacting with the real world again one by one the defenses went back up." So, what was the solution? Use Acid twice a day so you can stay spiritual?

"Denny, there has to be something other than drugs to give us the inner stamina to face life." I protested.

"Maybe," he admitted, "it would be nice but I don't know how realistic that is. Good luck on finding it; if you ever do you be sure to let me know, eh?"

Denny was far from being the only one among my associates using drugs for spiritual reasons. It was a rather common thought. That occultists used drugs to that end was no surprise but I was caught off guard when I heard what my friend "Jimmy the Joint," was doing. There hung on the wall in his den, a Certificate of Ordination from the Universal Life Church. It cost him all of ten dollars. He had a little group of followers who would gather at his house several times a week where they would sit cross–legged in a circle on his living room floor to "drop acid and trip out." That was church.

I became a strong advocate of abstinence and my stand on drug use was no secret to those around me, though they would argue the point, as did Bob Higgins who lived in Denny's commune with me.

"Max–think about it; you've read those prophecies in the Old Testament. I'm telling you those guys were on something," Bob would laugh mockingly. Of course, he would say that. Bob's business was drugs; he was the biggest drug supplier in town and dealt in them wherever he stayed.

"No the prophets weren't high on stuff," I would retort. "They were inspired by the Holy Spirit and seeing into another world."

"Suuuuuure!" would be his sarcastic reply.

"Come on now! The Bible teaches against drunkenness. And what is alcohol? It's just another drug?"

"It's a totally different thing."

"On no it's not! What's wrong with getting drunk? It messes with your reason—your sense of judgment. You do things when you're drinking you would never do otherwise. In fact, you do things you don't even remember doing. Things you later regret. And you know that the same thing is true for drugs."

"No, it's not" he resolutely resisted my logic, "if you drink you may get violent. But if you take drugs you'll sit in the corner starry eyed and stare out into space."

"Wait a minute! Haven't you ever seen a happy drunk? And what happened to the guys down in Houston I read about the other day. Three of them were having a glue sniffing party that turned into a massacre when one of them grabbed a machete and started hacking on the other two."

"I know. You hear those stories all the time!" Bob stamped his heavy iron ball handled cane forcibly on the floor several times, "but how do you know that they're true? They didn't happen at all I tell you. Those stories are purely fabricated lies from the establishment trying to squelch our freedom!"

"Bob, I have personally known some of those stories. Those ones aren't fabrications and nobody made them up! Besides, who needs the stories? Just look at the long—range effects of alcohol. How it wrecks your body. Anybody with any sense knows it's damaging to your health. And drugs are even worse. God wouldn't want people destroying themselves like that."

"Hey! He's the one who put them here!" Bob guffawed stamping his cane again.

"Who?"

"God."

"Put what here?"

"Drugs."

"And so what is your point?"

"I'm saying that they were His idea, not ours. If He put them here He must intend for us to use them."

"Oh, well, let's see," I put my finger to my chin "– Ok then. He put arsenic here too. Why don't we go out and find some of that and use it?"

Bob smiled, "Ah come on, Max. I'm sure He would have us use our common sense."

"What's senseless about using arsenic?" I asked.

"It'll kill you of course?"

"So will drugs and alcohol."

"Maybe alcohol but not drugs." Bob held up his index finger.

"You know better than that," I pointed at Bob. "Some of it is obviously damaging. The rest of it we haven't watched long enough to even know the long range effects."

"Your argument breaks down Max. Arsenic is immediate in its negative effects." Bob said.

"Exactly my point Bob! Just because we don't get immediate consequences we think we're getting away with something. But we aren't! It will catch up to us in time. You know it isn't the fall that hurts Bob, it's the stopping that kills you! Does it matter whether you commit suicide slow or fast? It's still suicide, either way."

Dennis, the founder of the commune butted in.

"Max, you above all people should be using acid. You are so spiritual and on such a quest for truth. You know that's the reason I invited you to stay here. You are the only guy I know who's spaced out on one book. You would get so much good from it."

"Dennis—you believe in a real devil and demons. Don't you see how I would open my mind to them if I took that stuff?" I asked.

"Did you ever stop to think that maybe it's them keeping you from it? Telling you lies so you won't discover the path into the kingdom of God? You know . . ." and here he quoted the Bible "*the kingdom of God is within you.*"

"Denny, I'm not going to find God in a pill."

"Why not?" he shrugged his shoulders.

"He's too big!" I said jokingly.

"Well you seem to be finding Him in a book—not much bigger you know!" The smart aleck grinned.

"No—the book is just a window into the universe of truth; and God is the ultimate Truth."

"Well—I'm just trying to turn you on. Far be it for me to force anything on you that you don't want."

"I would appreciate you letting me seek truth on my own terms Denny. I'm not forcing any of my stuff on you."

"Yeah, I know," Dennis said, half apologetically.

Bob had to get the last word in.

"Each to his own," he turned and hobbled away with his cane, as if I had missed a great opportunity.

But Bob didn't leave me to my own. That is not how it works. My not using drugs became an issue. It made me suspect. One day Bob took me for a ride in his Porsche. As we were driving through the country side on back roads, he spoke,

"You know Max, something's been going on at the commune."

"Really, what's that?"

"We've had some visitors showing up as if they were customers. But it's messed up."

"What do you mean?" I quarried.

"I'll just ask you outright. Have you been talking to anyone about our business?"

"What business?"

"Come on, don't play dumb Max."

"I don't know. Really."

"You know very well that we're selling drugs!"

"No," I said flatly, "I didn't know."

"Well it's obvious that someone knows. We've had nark agents come sniffing around. Someone's giving them information."

"Oh, I see. Since I choose to be drug free you think I'm the one telling them. Now I call that prejudice!"

"Who else?" Bob asked.

"Well it's not me," Was my reply.

By now we were in a remote place. Pulling over to the side of the road. Bob put the car into park and turned toward me in his seat,

"Well I hope not," he leaned toward me putting his face uncomfortably close to mine, and waving his cane's iron–balled handle in front of my face to punctuate his point and said, "because if we find out who it is it could be bad for their health."

I stammered, frightened that he might baste me with his cane on the spot.

"W–what do you mean?" I asked. Now I *was* playing dumb. I knew exactly what he meant.

"Well the people I do business with–you know–the mob? They don't like breaches of security. And they have ways of dealing with such things."

I laughed nervously. "Knock it off Bob. You know I wouldn't nark on you guys, even if I had known."

"Really?" He asked.

"Really," I responded.

"Like I said, I hope not," he repeated himself. Then lowering his cane he backed off, put the car into gear, and we drove away.

Soon thereafter I moved to another commune which, unlike the more exclusive one I had just left behind, was pretty much open to whoever wanted to stay. That one factor alone made my new home a crossroads for the bona fide hippy movement with its love ins, demonstrations, rock music, and of course drugs. It was called *The Lotus Palace*.

Soon after my settling into this new abode Bob Higgins came along and began hanging out there too. One night I compromised my stand against drugs and smoked some opium with him and a couple of girls. That might have been the one time when backsliding inadvertently worked in my best interest, for it was only a few days later, that I watched as paramedics carried Hank, the manager of my new commune, down the stairs from his second-floor room on a stretcher, a victim of drug overdose. As it turned out someone had spiked Hank's drink with enough cocaine to kill a horse. It was a miracle that he survived.

I knew, after the warning I had received, that it was more than coincidence that this happened just when Bob had made his appearance among us. He also disappeared like smoke right after the incident.

As I watched the paramedics disappear through the front door with Hank, I could see Bob in my mind's eye, half concealed in the shadows, leaning on his ebony cane, watching over the scene like a devil admiring his handiwork, the overdose a compliment of his vengeful wraith. I had no doubt concerning the connection. Bob probably thought Hank was snitching. I wondered if he got the benefit of a warning such as the one I had received. If I had not smoked the opium with Bob a few nights before, he would have probably thought it more than coincidence that I was present again when agents came poking around (if they did). I would probably have been at the top of his paranoid list of suspects with my drink being the one that got spiked. Oh the treachery of the pusher–man. Not everyone among us was about love and peace. There were serpents in our Eden.

The opium use with Bob was not the only time I went against my better judgment. I tried to maintain my conviction about not using drugs, but being part of an environment inundated with both them and their users made it difficult. The stuff was everywhere and everybody took it for granted that if you were in that environment, you were a user.

One night Tony and I were sitting cross–legged on the lobby floor of our local Greenwich Village style coffee house known as *The Berth*. I was sharing my conviction with him.

"I have sworn off drugs forever Tony–I'm done with them," I was saying.

"No kidding? I've come to the same conclusion. In fact I've been going to church lately." He said.

"Really? Where do you go?" I asked.

"I was raised Catholic so I've been going to St Bernard's."

Rita came along with a couple pieces of chocolate cake.

"It's Zack's birthday. Suzie baked him a cake. Want some?" she asked. We both accepted a piece and she moved on.

"Have you had anyone get down on you for not using yet?" I took a mouthful of the cake.

"Yeah, a few. But I figure I can find plenty of other friends who aren't into drugs. You having any problems?"

"I've had a few." I said, "But my biggest problem has been myself. Ever read the cartoon strip 'Pogo'?" I asked.

"On occasion. Why?" His cake was gone now.

"Well, one of Pogo's sayings seems to apply to me."

"What's that?"

"We have met the enemy—and he is us!" I wolfed down the last of my cake as we both laughed.

"I can identify with that," Tony said.

I stated my resolution. "I've backslidden a few times, but it's never been a good experience. I'll never do it again. I promise you that!"

"Well I'm done with them too," Tony declared boldly.

Then Rita came up again.

"How're you boys feeling?"

"Fine why?" Tony asked suspiciously.

"I was just wondering if you enjoyed the electric cake?"

"What? What do you mean *electric*?" I asked.

"Suzie baked it with enough marijuana in it to fly a mountain," She said as she flitted off like a butterfly.

Tony and I looked at each other with super–sized eyes.

"Oh well," he shrugged his shoulders, "Better luck next time, eh? We might as well just lean back and enjoy the ride."

"Maybe a change of environment would be in order," I suggested.

That was the end of our conversation. But my resolve was stronger than ever. I was going to quit drugs whatever it took!

But no matter how gallant my resolve I kept falling back occasionally. From the first time I had used drugs I desired their world of fantasy over the real one. The real world was much more painful and not nearly as exciting.

Another time I compromised my stand was the evening I was with the other members of Instinity and we all took a hallucinogenic drug. I have no idea what happened in the minds of the others but I entered into my fantasy world where I found myself sitting in the mouth of an enormous blue dragon that lay partly submerged in water. I was perched upon its tongue as if I were sitting upon a velvet throne. Around me the teeth of the dragon stuck up through the water like the breakers of a gigantic bay. Overhead hovered the top of the beast's mouth with its teeth hanging down like the stalactites of a cave. Looking over the bay I saw that it was covered with the scum, filth and mold of peoples' rotting dead bodies, some having deteriorated so far that they were nothing more than skeletons. The stench was so thick that it hung like a haze in the air and became entangled in my hair. The debris of many wrecked ships that was scattered over the surface of the water explained the corpses; they had made shipwreck on the breakers of the bay.

I looked out beyond the stalactites of the cave and past the breakers of the bay and was able to make out on the distant horizon a small ship. I watched with anticipation as the skiff drew closer to land wondering who was on board. I was finally able to squint my eyes and make out the same three boys who were actually with me in the room when I had taken the drug. There was Dave, Rick and Al in the boat heading for the breakers. Realizing that they would soon make shipwreck I cupped my hands over my mouth and began yelling at the top of my voice trying to get them to turn back. It was to no avail. They were unable to hear what I was saying and only drew closer to danger trying to make it out. I became frantic doubling my efforts to warn them. Soon the dragon around me began to fade. For a brief moment I was still in its' mouth and at the same time on a chair that began materializing beneath me. As I came to my senses I heard myself yelling to the others, "Turn back! Turn back—before it's too late.

Look, the breakers!" I saw Dave approach me as if he had walked across the waters of the bay.

"What's going on Max?" He asked.

"Can't you see the bay? The cave? Look at the stalactites!" I pointed upward.

He put his head next to mine and looked up trying to see what I was talking about.

Then I realized where I was; sitting in a living room chair in Dave White's house screaming at the others who were gathered around wondering what was wrong. But I didn't stop pleading,

"Turn back guys, turn back! Please don't follow me any further, I beg you! I'm just leading you into the mouth of the drug dragon. The demons are just dragging you to hell through my influence."

They looked at one another as if they couldn't understand me. And that was just the point; my life was speaking too loud for them to hear what I was saying. What garbled the message was my doings. I repented deeply of my drug use that night and confessed my fault to the others. I thought I was done with drugs forever, again.

For a while I moved back into my mother's place to get away from the drug scene. But I was still too close to the negative influences. The only people I knew were those who were like me or worse. I still fraternized with them but now was using the excuse that I was there to be, as Ronnie Garlow used to put it, a witness to them. I was clearly getting things out of sequence. How could I give away what I didn't possess myself? True, I was convinced of the facts of Christianity as far as I knew them but that was precisely the problem, I didn't know them very far. I had a measure of faith but I wasn't exactly sure what I was supposed to put my faith in. And I certainly had no concept of why Jesus had gone to the cross. How could I be a witness? I didn't even know what I was supposed to be a witness for. To be honest I don't think any of it mattered much to me because I wasn't being honest. All being a witness was to me at that point was an excuse to do what I wanted to do, which was be with my friends.

I went to one commune to share Jesus and the next thing I knew they had broken out the Acapulco Gold (a type of marijuana) and we went to smoking. What they didn't tell me is that it was laced with PCP (better known as *angel's dust*) which is a hallucinogen that, if you have the predisposition can push you over the edge into schizophrenia.

I sat on the floor in front of the stereo that was blasting out rock music and fixated on a set of drums that was setting immediately before me. Suddenly the high hat cymbals came alive and began going up and down on their own, in time with the music. Then the bass drum pedal began working itself. Soon the drums were all playing in perfect tempo with the melody that came from the speakers just behind me.

Before long the music drifted off into the distance and I couldn't hear a thing. Then my vision began to narrow in and soon the drums were blotted out. I went stone blind. As I sat in my dark, silent world all I could think about were things that terrorized me. Was my vision ever going to return? Was my hearing gone for good? How was I going to get out of this place if the police raided it. Soon all I could think of was Heaven and Hell, eternity and the judgment. I thought I had somehow overdosed or something and was on my way to meet God, and I knew I wasn't ready.

How can you overdose on pot? I asked myself. But it didn't matter. I couldn't deny that this was out of control. I began to pray desperately, promising God that if he would bring me down off of that drug and give me another chance I would serve him the best I knew how for the rest of my life and would never use drugs again. God was faithful! My vision returned quickly and that was all I needed to get out of the place. Next I began to hear again. But the paranoia remained and all the way back to my mother's house I kept looking over my shoulder, expecting the police to nab me at any moment and haul me away! Despite my fears, I got home safely that night and, true to my word, I began to get serious about serving the Lord the best I knew how. That was the last time I ever used drugs. That time I was done–and in more ways than one it was for good.

Like myself I found that God often convicted others of their drug use while under the influence of the drugs themselves. Any number of users have their stories to tell of their trip to hell or of encounters with demons while under the influence of drugs. One girl told me that she saw herself surrounded by fire with demons coming out of the flames clawing at her face then receding back into the blaze. I have heard a number of these stories but the most outstanding came out of the Lotus Palace commune I lived in which had what they called a *trip room*; a room specifically designed to enhance the drug experience. This young man's story punctuates the fact that while drugs promise to be *The Stairway to Heaven* they more often end up being *The Highway to Hell*. I will simply relate the story to you as it was told to me. The young man said,

"I got some pills from a friend. I didn't even know what they were, but he told me I would enjoy the high so I went to the trip room, sat on the floor with my back against the wall and swallowed one of the pills. Soon the wall in front of me became suddenly alive, breathing in and out like it was elastic or even flesh. It was the drug taking over. Then the wall turned into a large panoramic screen that wrapped itself around me. Next thing I knew the screen was literally dancing with swirling colors and patterns. Soon they began to change and the colors focused into a beautiful three-dimensional picture of the garden that stretched off into the distance as far as I could see.

"Intrigued by what I saw, I rose to my feet and walked up to the screen. I reached my hand out to touch its surface and found that it wasn't there. My hand went right through it. I waved my arm in the air in front of me and found that there was no surface to the screen at all! I stepped over what had been the boundary between the garden and myself and became part of my own hallucination. But this was as real as anything I had ever experienced. The garden was sun-lit and gorgeous. I saw species of flowers never seen by man before.

"Then my ears caught the strain of the most beautiful music I had ever heard. I turned my head in the direction from which it came and actually saw it floating through the air, as clear as a liquid. I wondered what could produce such an exquisite sound so I followed its trail. It led me to a concealed path in the garden which I followed. The further I went on the trail the more uphill and rugged it became. I was about to give up trying to find the music's source when I saw off in the distance at the top of the hill a beautiful set of gold and pearl gates.

"*It can't be!* I said to myself. *Those must be the gates of Heaven. I have got to get in!*

"I began to run. Then I felt my senses begin to reel. A backward pull gripped me. I lost my footing and began tumbling head over heels backward down the hill. Then falling into space, I landed on the floor of the trip room with its purple wall staring me in the face. The screen, the garden, the path, and the golden gates were all gone.

"'Wow!' I said out loud. 'I can't believe it! It's really true! This is the way to Life!'

"I decided to take a second pill. What if I got into heaven this time? I might discover the path to *Peace* and *Reality*! I sat impatiently waiting for the pill to work its magic.

"Soon I saw the screen again and the garden. Once more I entered my vision and found the path, which I followed, to the top of the hill. This time I entered through the gates of gold and into a world of splendor. I was overwhelmed with joy. Everywhere I looked I saw beautiful gardens that made the ones on the other side of the gate look like nothing. The aroma in the atmosphere was incredible. People clothed in white roamed everywhere leisurely all of them wearing an expression of complete serenity on their faces.

"Suddenly I noticed a big crowd of people off in the distance gathered around something. I stopped one of the by-passers and asked,

"'Pardon me sir, but can you tell me what's going on over there?'

"'Oh,' he said, 'you must be a stranger here.'

"Well, yes, I am," I told him, "But tell me, what's that going on over there?"

"Sure," he said, 'That's where God's throne is."

"'Really?' was all I said as I left him standing and I took off running. I had to see God!

"When I came to the edge of that crowd of people they parted before me like a living sea and I walked down that pathway like a king. The crowd began to cheer for me, thousands of them. It was like a homecoming. I had made it! I was in heaven! Coming to the base of the platform that God's throne sat upon I mounted the stairs. About half way to the top my ankle seemed to give way and my leg buckled beneath me. I found myself once more falling backwards into space, tumbling head over heels, and I landed on the floor in the trip room.

"I wondered if my last pill would produce the same results. I had no choice. I had to know. So again I swallowed the pill and waited. Once more I saw the screen, the garden, the path, the gates, and the crowd. Once more I received the welcome of royalty. And again, I climbed the stairs to God's throne.

"This time, as I neared the top, I saw the form of God come into view. I was stunned and stopped in my tracks, overwhelmed by such radiance and glory. Then God saw me and rose from His throne. Walking over to the edge of the platform He bent over, reached down, picked me up and held me in His arms."

"It was beyond description. I was at one with God! He sat back down on His throne with me on His lap and I just sat and gazed into the beautiful face of God."

"But I soon noticed changes starting to take place. God's countenance grew dim, and His smile turned into a frown. A cloud seemed to pass over His face and His eyes glistened, sending a chill through me. At the same moment, the color of His skin faded from a brilliant white to a colorless pale, then to a sickly ashen green. A blackened red began to flush into His features as if from the inside. The blue sky above was now swirling with dark churning clouds and lightening flashed. God began to tremble violently. I was terrified. Suddenly I noticed God's face beginning to sag. Next it started to run and flow until the melting flesh was dripping off the end of His chin. Soon I found myself sitting on the lap of a skeleton. I shrieked as I jumped from its dreadful lap and immediately I saw a bubbling around its feet as new muscles followed by new skin rolled up the skeleton's legs and body. Now the entire ground began to quake! Once the new skin and muscles had formed themselves into features I couldn't believe what I beheld. Before my very eyes,

God had turned into the devil himself! He rose from his fiery throne and opened his mouth in a deafening roar."

"Bolting from the platform I looked over my shoulder as I descended the steps and I saw satan throw back his head and let out a hellish laugh that shook the very foundations of hell. When I got to the base of the platform I looked around me for an escape route. Before there had been crowds of people in white robes singing the praises of God—now all there was to be seen were the souls of the damned screaming and crying. Before there had been angels worshipping God— in their place now were demons cursing, swearing, and blaspheming as they ran for shelter like cockroaches trying to escape satan's wrath. Before, there had been beautiful gardens but now there were only thorns and thistles. And before there had been a beautiful gold and pearl gate but now all I could find was a cast iron fence—and no way out! I was in Hell! I had to escape, I had to get out! Panic—stricken, I began running around frantically looking for a way of escape."

The young man went on to explain that in reality he was running around beating the walls of the trip room. He had had a bad trip, a freak-out.

I was rapidly learning that this young man's experience was not only the true picture of drugs but of all sin; for both promise to be the way to peace, satisfaction and enjoyment; the way to wring every ounce of enjoyment out of life, while in reality they turn out to be the way to a broken body, broken emotions, broken relationships and a broken mind.

The last I heard, the young man who told this story was still convinced that he was going to find his meaning to life through drugs. They tell me that as you speak to him his face constantly twitches from his continual drug use, and that in his coat pocket he always carries a piece of paper with his name and address on it, just in case he forgets who he is or where he came from; which he occasionally does.

While I do not think that drugs are the only things used by the demons known as *powers,* I am convinced that the drug culture is one of the main tar–pits of sin they have created in this world.

I continued to seek for God in spite of everything the principalities, powers, rulers of the darkness of this world and spiritual wickedness in heavenly places were throwing at me. It was only by the grace of God that I persevered.

Everywhere I turned it seemed that satan had his agents present to foil me in my pursuit of peace, but I was about to discover that God too has His agents in this world, and He was about to send one of them across my pathway.

CHAPTER 8

CONVICTION

The phone rang. It was Cheryl from three doors down on the other side of the street. Mom said she wanted to talk to me. Me? She was Mom's friend and old enough herself to be my mother. She and I had become casual acquaintances since I had moved back into my mother's house but what could she possibly want with me? Passing greetings and a few short conversations was the extent of our familiarity. I picked up the receiver,

"Hello."

"Hi Max. This is Cheryl. We're having a party down here," She began her explanation, "and we wondered if you could come down with your guitar and play some music for us?"

I thought it a bit strange but agreed anyway.

"Sure, I'll be there in a minute."

Cheryl was always friendly enough but she never showed the least bit of interest in music–particularly my kind. Even so I grabbed the 12–string *Stella* that Rick had left at my place and headed down the street.

Glad to have this I thought *it'll have more volume than any of our other acoustic guitars.*

Cheryl greeted me at her door and led me into the living room. After introducing me around she placed a folding chair in the middle of the floor and invited me to sit down. I did. Everyone else sat on couches, recliners and hassocks around the room with Stella and I in the center. I began cracking one–line jokes.

Good way to start, I told myself. *It'll break the ice.* We needed some ice breaking indeed. This was a conservative, previous generation crowd and they were all married couples.

They laughed at my jocularity and I laughed at their responses. Finally, a light red–haired fellow said,

"Could you play something for us."

And so I started with Donovan's *Catch the Wind*.

While everyone was focused on me Cheryl busied herself running back and forth between the kitchen and dining room carrying chips, dips, drinks, olives, and the like.

After a few more songs some of the guests began asking questions about the hippy movement. In response to one of my answers a large man said to the red–haired guest:

"See! I told you so!"

That response let me know that music was not the reason I had been invited to this party. This crowd wasn't after entertainment; they were after information about the hippy thing. No matter to me. I enjoyed letting everyone know that we were as human and harmless as they were.

Cheryl interrupted the conversation by clapping her hands to get attention as she walked into the middle of the living room.

"Time for refreshments," She announced. "Then some games!"

I lined up along with the others. The red–haired fellow that had called for songs was in front of me. He introduced himself as John.

"So, what are your thoughts about God?" he asked out of the blue.

"What about Him?" I asked, "I'm convinced that He's there."

"But how do you know that?"

I told him about my journey from atheism to the occult, from the occult to the Bible, and from the Bible to God. He asked what church I was part of.

"None." I told him, "all the churches my friends and I have tried didn't really believe the Bible."

"What do you mean?" he asked.

"For one thing, a lot of them don't believe God answers prayer. And almost none of them believe that there's a real spirit world—you know the devil and demons," I told him.

He laughed. I am sure I looked puzzled.

"Well they're not all that way," He explained.

"Really? You think you know some that aren't. I'd like to see them."

"My Father is a preacher. He takes the Bible literally. And so do I," John said.

"Oh, so you're a Christian?" I asked.

He stammered a moment then said, "Well, not exactly. But I'm a friend."

"A friend of who?" I inquired.

"Well," he hesitated as if struggling with how to say this, "The Bible and the church."

"Yeah, but what about Jesus? He said if you're not for Him you're against Him," I quoted from the Bible that John had just said he was a friend of.

"I know," he laughed to cover the awkwardness, "But I do believe the Bible to mean just what it says. And so does my father."

"Even if you do, my friends and I haven't found churches to be very receptive to outsiders; especially our type. Would your father's be any different?"

"You've got me there," he openly confessed. "I couldn't say that most of his churches would be any better that way."

"At least you're honest." I conceded. "But what's this about *churches*? Do you mean that he has more than one?"

"Well I mean the churches he preaches in. He travels and speaks in all types of them representing the work he's doing."

"And what kind of work would that be?" I wondered.

"He and my brother operate a rescue mission out in the country. They work with gutter alcoholics. In fact, it's made them a bit of an outcast themselves with many churches," John said. "They know what it's like to be an outcast, so you can be sure that at least my brother and dad would be receptive to you and your friends."

"Working with drunks makes them outcasts?" I was surprised that the church would reject her own.

"I'm afraid so Max. People are people whether in the church or out. Anywhere you have people they have their norms. If you fall beneath the norm they will punish you and if you rise above it they will persecute you. And the norm in many churches can be pretty narrow."

Trying my best to be subtle I cross–examined John attempting to catch him in his own words about prayer and the devil. He picked up on it but by then I had heard enough to know that John was genuine. Again, he assured me that his family believed the same as my friends and I.

Now that John had established some rapport with me I began to open up, particularly about my personal struggle with the discrepancy between the Bible account of creation and the theory of evolution. John proved to be exceptionally brilliant and challenged my thinking on a number of levels that night.

After the food, I left the party never expecting to see John again. But the next afternoon he called me.

"Hey Max, this is John, the guy you met at the party last night. I told my brother about you and he said he would like to meet you."

"Really? When?" I asked.

"Tonight, if he could," John said. "I'll bring him over to your place if it's alright,"

"Sure, come on over," I said.

Later that evening the doorbell rang. When I answered there stood John with a short, young looking redhead.

"Hi Max, this is my brother, Bruce"

"Hello," I replied, extending my hand.

"Pleased ta meet ya," Bruce responded as he grabbed my hand and shook it.

I invited them in and we sat around our dining room table.

"I told Max last night that you are a true Christian," John explained, looking at Bruce.

I thought to myself, *John can vouch for this guy all he wants but he's probably just like the rest.*

Then John explained to me that someone had asked Bruce to serve on a discussion panel at a convention about this new thing called *the hippy movement.*

"They thought that he was bound to know some in his line of work but he doesn't. So for several days now he's been asking everyone where he could find one." John continued, "he didn't get around to asking me until last night. I told him that I had, just by chance, met one earlier that very evening."

"So is this the brother you told me about?" I asked.

"Yes," John replied, "He's the one who started and runs the rescue mission I mentioned."

"So you mean he's the preacher?" I clarified.

"Yep, that would be him," John answered.

Bruce just looked at me and grinned.

I concluded that this was much worse than I had originally thought. If this Bruce guy was anything like the other professed Christians I had met it would be bad enough, but now that I realized he was one of their ringleaders I had next to no hope for him. *Might as well give him over to the devil* I thought.

Just the same I started putting Bruce through the test. I watched his reaction as I told him how the demons had been after my friends and me, giving him specific examples. He never missed a beat, agreeing with me on every point, then told me of encounters he'd had with demon powers in his line of work that were so incredible they made even my hair stand on end. With Bruce having passed stage one of the test with such flying colors I moved on to stage two; prayer. When I told him how God had been answering our prayers, he shared answers to prayer that sounded Biblical in proportion. They made our answers to prayer look like kindergarten stuff.

This guy is like a prophet who has dropped in on the twentieth century straight out of the Old Testament! I thought.

Shaking my head in amazement I said out loud, half to myself,

"There *is* a real Christian left in this world!" The brothers looked at each other incredulously. I addressed them directly,

"I've been telling my friends down at the coffee house that I was still holding on to a hope that there were some real Christians left in the churches. But they all insist that everyone in the churches is phony, plastic, and counterfeit. I told them that if there were counterfeits, then there had to be real ones to be counterfeited. They still aren't convinced. But you are my proof. I'm going to take you down there and prove to them that I was right!"

A look of concern swept down on Bruce's face like a dark cloud.

"Will they hurt me?" he asked.

"No, I don't think so," I laughed.

It was Saturday night when next we met. John wasn't with Bruce so just he and I went to the old converted theater on Johnson Street that now housed a Greenwich Village style coffee house called, *The Berth*. We entered the small room that used to be the ticket room but now served as an identification checkpoint. A bare blue bulb hanging by a cord from the ceiling dimly lit the room with blue walls and a few posters. There in the corner sat Stan on a bar stool sporting a sandy red goatee and mustache and wearing a denim jacket with the sleeves ripped out. He had dark sunglasses on despite the dimness of the room. He spoke,

"Hi ya Max. How ya doin'?"

"Fine" I answered.

"And who would this be?" He asked suspiciously with his face turned toward Bruce.

"Oh, this is a friend of mine. He's OK," I answered.

Not quite convinced, Stan probed further.

"Where'd you meet him?"

Bruce was getting uneasy so I cut to the quick.

"He's a preacher Stan. He wants to tell people here about God," I explained.

"Oh. Well then, if he's ok by you then that's good enough for me," Stan said. Taking the entrance fee from Bruce he stamped our hands and we passed on through the double doors into the lobby.

The carnival atmosphere inside had to be near to sensory overload for Bruce. The walls were painted in bright colors with a flashing strobe and a disco ball throwing swirling specs of refracted light all around the lobby. There was everything imaginable, from pretty Barb in her buckskin jacket and cowboy hat with her beautiful brown hair tumbling over her shoulders and her face completely covered with day glow paint of diverse colors and designs, to the attractive dark–haired Rita with her page boy haircut in her rather short skirted red dress who could have passed for an office secretary at work. The gamut ran all the way from Odd–Job who resembled a Viking to Jim in his three-piece suit. Fram walked by wearing a long black and purple striped stocking cap that he had stuffed with paper towels so that it stood about three feet straight up into the air with a tassel bobbing at its pointed end. His hair stuck straight out on both sides. If your mind hasn't conjured up an image already forget trying to picture it.

Bruce had a camera with him and asked Barb if he could take her picture.

"Sure!" she said loving the thought of it. Several others joined her for the photo shoot.

He continued taking pictures of anyone who would let him.

To the left, where the concession stand had once stood, was the head shop, the spot being subcontracted to a local enterprising young man who sold beads, jewelry, drug paraphernalia, clothes and posters. Refreshments were now purchased in a room further back.

We headed for the main auditorium being greeted by people as we went. Upon entering the large dark hall, we took a seat at one of the candle–lit round tables that filled the room where groups of two and three people were scattered throughout. At the moment, the small stage to the left that was generally used by the local entertainers, most of them folk singers, was empty, with only a dim blue light shining down on it. When the entertainment was local *underground* rock bands like *The Brambles* or *Morning Glory* they would perform on the large original stage up front. Right now, it too was empty. Instead of live performers music by the Indian satirist Ravi Shankar was being piped in over the sound system. Sitting on a stool behind a hung sheet in the middle of the main stage was a small glass ball that flailed revolving colors through its prismed sides which in turn threw incredible patterns over the entire back of the sheet that were equally visible from the front. It was an exact match for the music.

Bruce sat with his back to the small stage staring at the wall behind me. I turned around and looked at the large ceiling to floor mural painted on the wall in fluorescent colors. The two figures in it glowed under the black light. In front was the Zigzag man and behind him the top–hatted Geronimo from Chet Helme's Family Dog Productions logo. Both held marijuana joints between their fingers with the smoke from them forming the words overhead, "Mine Eyes Have Seen the Glory."

"Who are they in the picture?" Bruce asked.

"We'll talk about that later," I told him. "You stay here, I'll be right back."

"OK," He said as he anxiously looked around, then stood up and took a picture of the mural.

I ran off and found *Tork*. He was one of those that I had an ongoing debate with that there had to still be some sincere people in the churches that really believed what the Bible taught.

"Well I found one," I said as I walked up to him.

Tork turned around. "One what?" he asked.

"A sincere Christian who really believes the Bible!" I announced. Tork took the bait. He responded just as I expected.

"Well I'd like to see that!" He said, never thinking in this world that I would have the person with me in a place like this.

"Then follow me," I said as I turned to walk away. When we got back to the table I told Tork,

"Sit down. This man's a preacher, his name is Bruce and he wants to talk to you about God!"

Bruce started in. Tork being quite an intellectual I knew that this was going to take a while so I went in search of someone else. By the time I got back Bruce had asked Tork about the mural on the wall and he had convinced Bruce that the people in it were Jesus Christ and John the Baptist smoking marijuana. Now he was trying to tell Bruce that the prophets' visions in the Bible were drug induced. But despite all the head games Bruce was much more than holding his own. His surprisingly simple logic was more than a match for Tork's intellectual gymnastics.

When Tork declared that the Bible contradicted itself Bruce whipped a New Testament out of the inside pocket of his jacket. He held it out to him and said,

"Where? Show me, because I want to know. I've heard that before and after studying this thing pretty intensely for years I can't seem to find anywhere that it does that."

"Well everybody knows that it does," Tork stammered.

"I don't. So help me out. Show me where?" Bruce pressed the point.

"Well I don't know where, but I've been shown before," He insisted.

Bruce let Tork off the hook,

"Well the next time you see whoever showed it to you have them give me a call," he said offering a business card to Tork.

"Maybe he can help me find where it contradicts itself."

Here Bruce stopped for dramatic effect and acted as if he were thinking then giving me a knowing look said,

"Or maybe the problem is that it contradicts them."

Tork toned down for a moment. I took advantage of the lull in the conversation to introduce Rita.

"Bruce this is Rita, Rita–Bruce. Sit down here! Bruce is a preacher, and he's a *real* Christian. He wants to tell you about God!"

Bruce started telling Rita that because God answers prayer we can be assured that there is a God. It wasn't long before others began to saunter up to the table and listen to the now three–way conversation that was getting louder by the moment. Soon quite a crowd had gathered and dialogue was freely flowing between Bruce and several others.

With the passing of a few more minutes Bruce was on his feet doing the closest thing I had ever heard to preaching without it seeming like it was. All fear appeared to have left him.

Then came the owner, skinny Vic, looking like a college prep from Yale with his pullover sweater and conservative haircut.

"Wait! Stop! Quit! Hold everything!" He was yelling as he pushed his way through the crowd. When he got to the center he leveled his eyes on Bruce and asked:

"You're a preacher, aren't you?"

"How'd you guess?" Bruce responded. Vic smiled taken back by the boldness of this sawed-off runt.

"Do you know what I'm going to do?" Vic asked in return.

"No," confessed Bruce supposing that he was about to be tossed out of the place.

"I'm going to give you a special room upstairs where you can talk to these young people. Bring all the church people you can get to come, and as many of these young people as you can help–good for you!"

Bruce took Vic at his word. The next time he came he brought a vanload of church people. And the next time several carloads. Eventually he was bringing caravans of cars.

Vic gave Bruce's group free use of what used to be the projector room of the old theater. Every Saturday night we would all make our way up the narrow set of stairs and cram into what the Christians dubbed, *The Upper Room*. Most of my friends were loaded with questions, some of them being sincere and others more mocking than not. Many of them argued, debated, fumed, and fussed with the Christians while the Christians just kept testifying, praising God, reading from the Bible, praying, exhorting, singing and answering questions.

On one occasion Bruce brought his slide projector and showed the slide presentation of his mission work that he used everywhere he went. One of the most recent additions to the presentation was at the end. It was a group of pictures of his new work with the hippies. It started with a picture of some friends and I, taken the day we made the trip into the country to see the rescue mission. This was followed by the pictures he had taken on his first trip to the Berth. People made all kinds of comments and laughed as each other's pictures came up. When Bruce got to the picture of the wall mural someone said,

"Look! He got Craig's Zig–Zag man!"

"Who?" Bruce asked.

"The Zig–Zag man," someone else answered.

"Who's that?" Bruce wondered.

It was Barb who answered. "He's the emblem of the company that makes the cigarette papers everyone uses to smoke pot."

"Someone told me that it was a picture of Jesus and John the Baptist smoking marijuana." Bruce was consternated.

"Well they were just pulling your leg. Look," Barb said as she pulled a pack of banana flavored Zig–Zag papers out of her fringed purse and showed them to him.

"Do you know that I take these slides with me all over the country showing them to people as I represent my mission work?" Bruce asked.

"And let me guess," Barbara said, "You've been telling them that this was a picture of John the Baptist and Jesus smoking marijuana."

"Yep!" Bruce answered.

Everybody roared with laughter. Bruce hung his head and slowly shook it as he said,

"I'm just glad you let me know before I told the other half of the world."

My friendship with Bruce continued to grow throughout the summer that year. He as well as some of his preacher acquaintances visited my friends and I in our communes and even in my home. They were very accepting and non-condemning. A highlight was when Bruce's father George brought his accordion and came to one of the communes I stayed in. He sat on a chair in the middle of the living room, pumping the thing and telling stories until my friends were nearly rolling on the floor with laughter. George had been an entertainer in vaudeville working closely with greats like Rudy Vallee and Marshall Jones (aka Grandpa Jones—he was also from Akron) and really knew how to handle a crowd. Being straight from Scotland and having a heavy brogue made him even more of a curiosity to everyone. And being converted from show business he knew how to entertain a crowd and just when to make a jab with the truth to get a point across. They were all delighted with him.

I began to occasionally go to church with Bruce when he was speaking, beginning with the convention that had originally sent him on his search for hippies. After the discussion panel, several of my friends and I stood on the platform with Bruce and answered questions about the hippy movement.

Bruce began inviting me to travel with him when he was going out to represent his mission work. Employing the original format, we had used at the convention he would have me join him behind the pulpit near the end of the service to field questions.

Traveling together, sometimes for hours on end gave me a lot of time to ask Bruce questions about the Bible and the Christian faith. I noticed that everywhere we went he requested prayer for God to move upon the peoples of the Berth. I don't know of anyone, other than myself, who was privy to the information on both sides of that story. It does seem that those prayers were heard. It is my assessment that in the end they prayed the place clear out of business.

During this same time, I began to see that following Jesus involved a price. But not the kind of price you pay for a commodity on a shelf in a store. I had before declared that I was on a quest for peace and that I would go to any extreme to get it once I knew where it was to be found. Now I was convinced that peace could only be found in Jesus. I saw the desired object. It was within my grasp. I also saw that what I was after was free, at least for me, and at least monetarily; but it was not cheap. It was neither cheap for the one who purchased it for me nor would it be cheap in what I would have to endure in its return. There was indeed an extreme to which I would have to go if I was to have it and hold on to it. Thus, I saw that there was a price tag dangling from the prized possession. So walking up to it I took the tag in hand and saw there written the cost. It said "*Everything!*"

At first I wasn't quite sure what *everything* meant. But over the next while God clarified the meaning. As it began to come into focus I dropped the tag and began backing away saying,

"Well now, I didn't quite mean *that!*"

Just as when satan had earlier made an appeal for me to surrender my all to him, so I now came to understand that God was asking for the same thing. It made me uncomfortable. I felt insecure giving control of my life over to another, even if it was God. Through the years, I had gotten used to being in charge of my own life. But then, on the other hand, I saw that I wasn't doing such a great job of running my own show anyway. I was pretty much running it into the ground. All the same I was too self–centered to give myself over to anyone else's complete command; and in the Lord's case, I knew that it was going to have to be everything or nothing at all.

I began feeling uneasy about specific things in my life. I came to recognize the anxious sensations as a kind of inner voice that would kick up on occasion if there was some area of my life that the voice thought I needed to bring into line. It was uncanny the way the Christians around me would say and do things that confirmed the voice. It was like they were in league with each other. But there was no way that they could so frequently know exactly what the voice inside my head had been saying.

An example was when the inner voice began to suggest that I quit playing with Istinity. Not that I thought of the music itself as being wrong but as a career it seemed problematic for me. There was a lot more "stuff" that went with that territory than I seemed to be able to handle. But at the time music was the only plan I had for my future. In fact it was my life, and more to the point it was my esteem. It was, in essence, everything. And it was there that I met my spiritual Waterloo. However long a shot it may have been, I could not bring myself to the point of willingly giving up this dream to follow somebody else's path. I had a suspicion that I might be asked to enter the ministry.

Ever since I had discovered there was a spirit world I had anticipated that it might come down to that. I had asked a Lutheran priest how I was to know if I was supposed to preach. He said that I would receive a call from God if that was the direction I was supposed to go. I thought I might be hearing it now. The prophetic aspect of such a thing had appealed to me initially, but I now found myself vacillating, unwilling to make the necessary sacrifices to pursue such a calling.

While I was wrestling with this issue several area churches that were connected to Bruce's rescue mission sponsored a tent meeting on the mission's grounds. They called it the LSD (Lord, Savior, Deliverer) Crusade. During an afternoon service at this crusade I sat on a folding chair in the middle of the tent as Bruce was preaching although I couldn't have told you what about. But for just a moment something riveted my complete attention on him, with everything else around me fading completely into the background. In that one moment Bruce pointed straight at me and piercingly asked,

"Are you selling your soul for music?!!"

Immediately my heart jumped into my throat and began palpitating loudly. I felt like some kind of covering had just been ripped away. I was exposed!

How could he possibly know that? I wondered. *I haven't told anybody about it. How could he even think of such a thing? Nobody in his world would ever have that kind of a problem.*

After the meeting, I quickly made my way to Bruce to interrogate him.

"Have you ever heard of God talking to anybody about music?" I asked.

"No," he answered, "what do you mean and why do you ask?"

"Well, you know, since you mentioned it in your preaching I thought maybe you had," I said.

"What are you talking about, Max? I didn't say anything about music while I was preaching," He declared.

"Sure, you did. And you pointed right at me."

"Did not!"

"Yes, you did! I thought you were preaching right at me!"

"Humph! Never!" said he, "I preach by inspiration not information. I never watch my sermons walk in the back door. I just listen to the Spirit and that's what I preach."

"So you weren't just preaching at me?" I asked again.

"Absolutely not!" he insisted. "If I have something to say to you personally I'll tell you one on one. I think it's cowardly to pretend to be speaking to a crowd when you're really just saying something for the benefit of one person."

I was still doubtful. My skepticism was fueled, at least in part by my own internal guilt. Every time I got around these Christians I felt overwhelmed with shame. It was like they somehow knew all the appalling things I had ever done that were wrong; the things that even I did not want to know or think about. And the most recent ones were right on the top. I was sure they could see them.

I began making what I thought were steps toward a laying down of arms. In reality they were only concessions. They were things I was willing to sacrifice if God would leave the other things alone. In essence they were decoys.

Ok! I was willing to give up drugs. So what–I had already committed to that. Alcohol was no big deal. Well of course it wasn't–I didn't drink any more. Waiting until I was married for intimacy with my future wife was reasonable. I knew I would have a struggle with it but I had already concluded that sex was over–rated anyway. I was sure I could wait. The lifestyle many of my friends engaged in held no real appeal for me either. As for my friends themselves–now that was a little harder. I needn't have worried about giving them up though. I found out soon enough that they weren't the friends I had thought them to be. As my life began to change they started falling away like the scabs from chicken pox fall off kids. They just quit coming around. So I would go look them up. They almost universally started with a similar question like,

"Hey Max buddy! Where have you been?"

I would reply,

"What do you mean where have I been? I've been the same place I've always been. How come I've had to look you up the last five times?"

They all forsook me. Real friends don't do that! It hurt but–Oh well. I could make new friends I guessed; but give up music? That was beyond all reason.

Another of the specific things the inner voice put its finger on was hanging around the Berth on the weekends. But once again I was being obstinate about doing things my own way. I even declared that it had to be God Who made the opportunity for me to contract with Vic, the owner, to do some promotional artwork. I convinced myself that it was God's way of supplying for my financial needs. God apparently decided that it was time to take things to the next level since I wasn't listening to the inner voice. It's rather a bit like children; if they won't listen to the warnings of their parents there comes a point when it's time for something more than talking.

One Saturday night I took some artistic proposals to Vic in a folder and we picked out a couple of final designs for me to work on. That night several of us stayed for an after–hours party when the place closed at midnight. It was 2:00 A.M. on Sunday morning, after several of my friends and I left for home, the building not yet being out of sight, that a carload of those precursors to the rednecks, known to us by the name *greasers,* drove by. As often would have been the case on an early Sunday morning with these monomaniacs whose culture was poles apart from our own. They had been drinking.

One of them hurled a profane insult out the back window as the car drove by. A drive–by hooting I guess you would call it. With it being against my very temperament at that time, I have no idea why I did it, but before I realized what was happening my mouth had flown open and an equally profane insult had come out, which I flung after the car as it went down the street. Almost instantly the brake lights lit up. I knew in that dreadful moment that I had made what might turn out to be a fatal mistake. The car turned itself around and came racing down the street with the engine roaring and the headlights glaring. The machine came to a screeching halt, and all four doors flew open. Out of each there jumped a gigantic thug, four in all. We scattered like the chickens we were. Down the alleys and driveways, we ran, through back yards and over fences. One of the boys with us was even afflicted with a measure of cerebral palsy and we had to half carry him. I don't know how, other than by divine intervention, but we managed to escape.

You'd have thought that I would have learned something that night. I should've been able to figure out that I needed to stay away from the Berth as the inner voice had been prodding me. But no, not clueless me! So the very next Saturday night found me once again at the Berth. I rationalized to myself that I had to go finish the negotiations with Vic about the artwork. We were to settle on the final product that night. Why it would be downright irresponsible to not go. It's pretty easy to justify what you already want to do any-way. I took a folder with several finished pieces for Vic to decide from. When I left that night, our plans were finalized. All I had to do now was show up next week with the finished product and collect the cash.

That night there was another after–hours party for which I stayed. You know, you have to take part in all the incidental social functions when you are doing the kind of work I was. After leaving the place Sunday morning, again about 2:00 A.M. as several of my friends and I were once more on our way home, on the opposite side of the street but at the same identical spot as the week before, another carload of *greasers* came by. And of course, they had been drinking. Once again one of them yelled something insulting out the window at us. You would have thought I'd have learned not to do it by the previous week's experience, but my mouth involuntarily flew open and out came another affront. The taillights of the car lit up. The car turned itself around and came racing back down the street with the engine roaring and the headlights glar-ing. The car came to a screeching halt and all four doors flew open. Out jumped four gigantic thugs. *You've got to be kidding! This should only happen in a book,* I thought to myself as we took off again! Down the alleys and driveways we ran, through back yards and over fences.

I suppose all would have gone well had we been on the other side of the street–we had learned that escape route the week before. But this time one of my friends and I got into a yard that was fenced in with no appar-ent way out. We crouched in the dark behind the cor-ner of the garage. All four brutes were coming down the driveway casting long shadows before them from the streetlight. They couldn't see us but they knew we had gone down that driveway. It would only be a matter of time until by process of elimination they would locate us and make mincemeat out of us in a twinkling.

Then I had an *Aha! Moment*, better known in religious circles as an *epiphany*. I suddenly realized what was happening. This two-by-four brain of mine put two and two together and amazing as it may seem it added up to four! This was God's louder way of speaking to me about not going to the Berth. I said to my friend,

"I'm pretty sure I know what's going on. I think I can get us out of this."

"Then hurry!" he urged.

I bowed my head and began talking to God.

"What are you doing?" my friend whispered.

"Shhh! I'm praying!" I said.

"We're about to be killed and you get religious?"

"No atheists in foxholes," I declared, repeating Ronnie Garlow's line then went on praying.

"I'm gettin' outta here," He said.

With that he leaped over the fence behind us getting his foot caught in the process. Down he went on the other side, head first. Scrambling to his feet he fled off into the darkness. The ruckus got the henchmen's attention. They looked right at the noise and so, right at me. Though I knew they couldn't see me it was still unnerving. They continued walking down the driveway right toward me.

Then I prayed in my heart and told the Lord that if He would get me out of this I would never go back to the Berth again.

"What about the artwork you have to deliver next week?" the voice inside of me seemed to ask. I didn't answer by words. I simply opened my folder with all the artwork in it and threw the papers into the air.

It is no exaggeration. All four of those men stopped as instantly in their tracks as if they had brake shoes on their feet. They turned around immediately, went back to their car, got in, closed the doors and drove away. And of course, I never did go back to the Berth again. Sorry Vic, but artists like me are a dime a dozen anyway–just ask Linda! You were probably just being patronizing anyway. I hope whoever found the art-work in their back yard enjoyed it.

I had a growing understanding that the only way I could make the changes the inner voice was telling me was necessary (and by now I knew it was true) was to walk away from everything I knew, including the sub-culture I was a part of, and start life over again some-where else. That is not true for many people but it was for me.

I knew that it was in everyone's best interest that I do so. I had justified my staying in the subculture by telling myself that I needed to be a witness to those who were a part of it. But I wasn't stable enough to be of any help to them in my current condition. The most likely way I would ever be able to help them was to take some time out and get my own head screwed on straight. I knew I could help no one any more than I had been helped myself.

Since I had given up The Berth I decided to take things a little further in appeasing the inner voice that was troubling me by making an attempt to leave Istin-ity. I secretly hoped that the others would talk me out of it but to my surprise by mutual consent we drew up a treaty that negotiated a temporary suspension of the band.

During the same time we were arranging to part ways I moved back into the Lotus Palace commune, where Hank, the Palace's manager, came up with a business proposal. He spoke to several of his friends about putting together a new band, which he would manage. He approached Dave who had played bass for Istinity and who was also living at the Palace at the time about playing with the group. Dave suggested that they might want to consider me for another guitarist. So we both became part of Hank's *Blind Thomas* named originally after famed blues legend, Blind Lemon Jefferson, only we didn't want to use Jefferson because it was already taken by San Francisco's *Jefferson Airplane*, so we went with the first name of another well–known Jefferson–Thomas Jefferson. We were three guitars and a bass with a drummer, our specialty being long unbroken intervals of music. We were kind of what they called a *jam band*.

Hank was well connected and in no time at all got us a gig to open for the English band *Pink Floyd* who was going to be playing that upcoming July at the *Fifth Detention* in Ann Arbor Michigan. It was far enough ahead of time for us to get some stuff together. He also was able to land financial backing for us to record an album. Professionally things seemed to be looking good.

Not many days later, as *The Blind Thomas* was practicing in the basement of the Lotus Palace, a depression of demonic proportions settled over me. I had suspected for some time that I had a chemical imbalance that was responsible for the bouts of depression I had been experiencing, but I also discovered later that a local witch's coven had been using the same basement we were practicing in for satanic rituals and worship services. The latter may have played as big a role, if not a bigger role in my depression than the organic problem did. *I can't stand this any longer* I thought to myself. During a break I laid my guitar down and said to the others,

"Boys, I'm going out for a walk."

Outside it was late night. I began to walk around the block. The thought of suicide came into my mind.

It was far from the first time it had presented itself to me. But this time it caught me at emotional low ebb. I decided then and there that this depression was too painful for me to bear any longer. Even something as radical as death seemed to be a welcome escape from it. I thought of a bridge in the area and as if drawn by some magnetic force I headed toward it. As I grew closer I made up my mind that when I got there I was going to throw myself off of it.

Why not? I was crazy anyway. The army had confirmed it. Ever since then I had felt like I was losing grips on sanity and had become increasingly preoccupied with the thought of death. I had become convinced that my end was to be committed to a psychiatric hospital and spend the rest of my days there, forgotten by the world until the time of my departure from this life. I thought I was powerless over this destiny. But here was a way I could take control. I could end it myself; *right then!* Crazy logic I knew, but I was immensely confused.

When I got to the foot of the bridge there was an alley that ran off to the left. Most likely because of my fears, and especially the thought of hell, I turned into the alley to avoid the bridge. As I walked down that brick backstreet I looked up at the dark sky and sparkling stars. I wondered if there was a God out there. The heavy oppressive presence that smothered me told me that there was no One. I spoke into the air just in case. It was a single, one-word prayer. But in that one word I poured out my entire soul.

"Why?"

I groaned: It was more of a pitiful whine than a prayer.

I suddenly sensed the presence of the same Spirit I had often felt before. I knew without a doubt that this was the God whose existence I had just questioned. A thought came into my mind so strong that it may as well have been an audible voice.

"If you'll go pray I'll tell you why," It said.

I went to the park across the street from the commune and got into the middle of a clump of bushes. There I began to pour my heart out to God. A Holy presence settled down on that shrubbery and the same strong voice spoke again.

"Max, I've told you that you can't be a Christian and hang around these people. It's not that they are worse than anyone else, it's just the wrong environment for you. You are not strong enough to take my message to them right now. You need to go get yourself spiritually established, and then come back when I tell you to. Besides I have greater plans for you and a great many more people for you to share your message with. I have plenty of other people I can use to reach your friends anyway. You can trust them to me"

"But where will I go?" I asked. "My Mother's place is no escape from all this. It's not far enough away! If I go there everybody will be beating the door down looking for me."

"Call Bruce and go to his mission," The voice suggested.

"He can't have me there," I told the voice. "That's a rescue mission for winos not people like me."

But the voice said no more. That was the end of the communication. But it was all I needed. I went back to the commune and forgetting the *Blind Thomas* climbed into my alcove off the trip room and fell into a deep and restful sleep as if it were a gift from God.

When I woke the next morning, I made my way to the nearest phone booth and spent my last dime to call Bruce. I told him what had happened and he said,

"Hallelujah! I've been praying and fasting for this day! I'll be in to get you within an hour."

In less time than that Bruce showed up riding a motorcycle. I wasn't able to take much with me but I wasn't going to need much from my past where I was heading. *If you're traveling far, travel light* is what I had always heard. Little did I know that I was stepping onto the conveyor belt to my future. I would never return to The Berth, The Lotus Palace or Instinity again. The only way I would return to that city at all for the next two decades was as short sorties into enemy territory. I did however eventually get a chance to share the gospel with many of my closer friends. In fact, a number of them came to hear me preach in church.

For the rest of my generation my leaving was so clean cut that for them I just dropped out of sight, never to be heard of again; at least not for the next 30 years. By then some of them had tracked me down and made contact with me at which point I attended the only reunion our graduating class ever had. It was the year we all turned 50. During the proceedings, I was introduced as the "original wildcat" (our school mascot) and got to share my story with them. To my amazement, a number of them had become Christians. I also prayed with the group several times. But now it's time for the rest of the story.

CHAPTER 9

COMING TO MYSELF

When I first stepped foot on Bruce's rescue mission grounds I was immediately taken with the outstanding stories behind many of the men. The number of residents constantly fluctuated but there were around 70 of them at any given time; some of them transients or occasionals but nearly three–fourths of them mainstays. Among these was Steve from Russia who wired one of the first rockets that ever pierced the heavens; he was an electronic genius. Then there was Fred who had been a pharmacist and Tim who had been an actor, while Sam was an ordained minister and Peter a licensed undertaker. Walter once worked as an executive for The Goodyear Rubber Corporation and George was a plasterer by trade. Tennessee had been a constable in his home state, and Dale dropped out of college only eight hours away from his medical doctor's degree. Raymond had made a career out of the army attaining unto the rank of sergeant, while Emil had been a lumberjack, Euwell a factory worker, and Denton a professional boxer.

With the men coming from all cultures and religious backgrounds, the mission, like America, was a virtual melting pot; it was an education just being around the men.

None of the stories were any more outstanding than Jack Christy's. As a child Jack had lost his left leg jumping a freight train. His extended convalescence created a need for outlet so Jack began taking piano lessons. With plenty of time for practice and a natural skill for the endeavor he excelled at the keyboard. Once he became an adult Jack pursued music as a career and in time rose to the top of his profession becoming a well–known concert pianist. When you heard him play you knew it to be true. Nobody could have that level of skill or that command of their instrument without higher education and much experience. Jack, having attained command of his own orchestra began playing in dance halls across America, criss-crossing paths with the likes of Glenn Miller and Lawrence Welk. He and his orchestra later provided entertainment for passengers on an ocean liner between America and Europe. But Jack claimed that his gift became his curse, because people would continually set drinks on the piano and ask for more music. One drink lead to another and eventually Jack became a gutter alcoholic and lost everything. For years he would occasionally gather himself out of the gutter and wander into a downtown store in Akron where they sold pianos, place himself on a bench and start playing one of the instruments. Of course, he gathered a crowd every time. Salesmen would slip Jack a few dollars for drawing prospect in for them which he would use to get on his next drunk. I don't know if it was the traumatic blows of the life he had chosen or if he had come to his conclusion earlier in life, but Jack was a confirmed and cynical atheist.

The first time Jack saw me walking across the mission grounds he was standing with Bruce's brother–in–law Ron. He spoke,

"Now there is a young man who will never amount to a hill of beans."

"Why do you say that?" Ron asked.

"Because. Look at him. Look how he walks, all hunched over. He's spineless. He doesn't have an ounce of character or discipline in him," he said.

Boy, talk about prejudging. The sad thing is that he was dead on. He had me pegged to a tee. I might fool some people but never the ever–perceptive Jack Christy. Left to myself I never would have amounted to a hill of beans. In fact, I am quite secure in the opinion that I never have developed as far I should have. But I also have to humbly confess that I am a long way down the road from where I began. And best of all–*I am still going*. The only reason I have gotten as far as I have is because of an intervening event. Due to that one thing, I do believe that I may have been worth at least my beanage in life! That event is what this chapter is about. And because of the same event Jack, years later, made his way back to Ron and reminded him of that conversation and said,

"Well I don't say it often but I was wrong; about Max I mean. I don't know what happened to that young man but something radically changed him!"

Ron had the key.

"Jack," he said "the problem is that you left God out of the equation. Never underestimate what He can do with someone."

Now that makes me want to shout all the way to the beanery! Beanage notwithstanding, I guess I was at least a testimony to Jack.

10 years before I came on the scene Bruce had been sitting in the college library where he was studying for the ministry waiting for the first class of his second year to start. He had been praying and fasting for a discernment of God's plan for his life throughout the summer months. Now as he sat at the table he unexpectedly received an epiphany in the form of a mental picture. The image of a wino lying in a gutter flashed through his mind as vivid as a photograph and at the same moment Bruce declares God spoke to him as clear as if it had been an audible voice.

"I want you to leave this place and go work with alcoholics."

Bruce stood to his feet, walked up to a friend at the next table and handed him his books.

"Would you turn these in for me when the office opens?" he asked.

"Why? Where are you going?" the student wondered.

"I'm leaving. God has just called me to work with alcoholics." Bruce explained.

"You can't do that!" the boy said.

"Keep both eyes on me." Bruce challenged him as he walked out the door and went home.

After telling his father George that God had called him to work with alcoholics, George said,

"If that is what God is calling you to do then don't you dare do another thing."

George had been praying for and working with alcoholics for years. He felt honored and considered it an answer to prayer that God would call his son to establish a permanent work doing the same thing.

The two of them found a suitable building in downtown Akron but George said,

"You better let me talk to the owner. You look a little young to be trying to rent a place like this."

"When George talked to the man and explained what they wanted to do, the man said,

"I'll tell you what. For a project like that, I'm willing to rent it to you for $50 a month."

"Praise the Lord!" George shouted.

Startled, the man asked, "Why'd you say that?"

"For giving us a good price!" George exclaimed.

"Well, for taking that attitude I'm going to give it to you rent–free for the first 6 months."

For several years, the mission operated out of that building but eventually the city of Akron decided to clean that part of town up and condemned every building on the block and scheduled their demolition.

George contacted a real estate agent he knew who brought a building to their attention that was situated on an eight and a half–acre tract of land five miles outside of the city. The main building was a large three–story structure that had originally been built to be a church. But before it was finished the pastor died and the congregation sold it to a man who turned it into a bar, dance hall, and house of prostitution. It was known far and wide as *the Lazy L Ranch*. Three men had been murdered in the building.

Half way across toward the other side of the property the same man had moved a small camper trailer to live in it. He eventually added a room, then another and then another. Ultimately the camper got swallowed up inside the house. From the outside, you couldn't even tell it was there. It was a strange experience to be walking through the place then suddenly step into a room and find yourself in a mid-1940's era camper trailer. Last I knew it was still a part of the house's inner structure.

Later when this man was arrested for his crimes and sent to prison the property was foreclosed on by the bank and scheduled for auction.

That was when the place was brought to the Hawthorn's attention. Upon visiting the property Bruce and his dad thought the place was perfect but didn't think they could ever afford it. Kneeling on the main floor of the large building they asked God that if it was His will He would give them the place. They felt impressed to offer $6,500.

"Oh, that will never touch it," their real estate agent told them.

"Well that's what we believe the Lord wants us to offer and if He wants us to have it we'll get it for that price." George told him.

At the auction the opening bid was made by a local businessman for $9,500. When nobody else present offered to bid, the auctioneer turned to Bruce and George's real estate agent and said,

"Mr. Taylor, I thought you had someone who was interested in the building."

"I do," he said. "It's a couple of preachers, but all they can afford is $6,500. In fact they had to borrow that."

"Oh well," said the auctioneer dismissing the matter, and then added as an afterthought, "What would a couple of preachers want with an old bar anyway?"

That was when Mr. Taylor rose to his feet and said,

"Oh, I can tell you what they want to do with it. They want to start a rescue mission for alcoholics," and proceeded to tell all those present about the Hawthorn's work.

The auctioneer thought for a moment then looked at the bank president who was present.

"Go ahead and sell it to the preachers. The bank will take a loss." The president said.

Then turning to the first bidder the auctioneer asked, "Would you like to withdraw your bid?"

The businessman instantly responded, "Yes I would!"

Immediately the auctioneer slammed his gavel down and said "Sold to the preachers for $6,500!"

So the Hawthorns bought the property and God miraculously sent the money in to pay the loan off within a very short while. The story from then on was one of miracle after miracle.

And so, they turned the place into the *Barberton Rescue Mission* naming it after the closest suburb of Akron. Bruce felt that the building's story paralleled many of the men's lives. Like the building, they too had a good start in life but had gone astray. Now at the Barberton Rescue Mission they were coming back to God.

I will have to forever thank God for having these men start their work. It became my redemption center, ministry launching pad and home. Going there has always been like going home for me.

Bruce didn't think it wise to put me with the other men in the first-floor dormitory of the main building until he saw how we got along. He was afraid the age and cultural gap would instigate conflicts if we got too close. So I took up residence in an old one–room wood heated shack behind the house Bruce and his wife Phyllis lived in.

They put one of the most eccentric people I have ever known in it with me. I guess they thought he would be a positive influence. Emil Matson aka *The Axeman* (he had been a lumberjack) was a converted alcoholic. Being over sixty years old when he became a Christian he felt that he had wasted most of his life and asked God what he should do with what was left. Feeling impressed that God had called him to memorize scripture he came to be called *The Walking Bible*. Emil had over a thousand chapters of the King James Version of the Bible committed to memory. Since there are only 1189 chapters in the Bible he had most of it in his head. Some of it he would quote word for word– backwards! You could open the Bible at random and start reading and within a few words he could stop you and tell what book, chapter, and verse you were at. In fact, he could stop you and start quoting, word perfect, where you had left off. What an inspiration he was. But he was so eccentric that his influence was pretty much nil. At least he didn't do me any harm, and he was certainly entertaining to be around.

The buildings all had names. Matson's and mine was *the Brown House* because of its color. Bruce and Phyllis's was *the Tin House*, because it was completely covered with corrugated sheet metal. The three–story building across the property, which housed The Mission proper, was appropriately called *the Big House*. The shed where the men went and sat around a pot-bellied stove, told stories and smoked was dubbed *the Smoke House*.

Bruce and Phyllis agreed together to have me eat with them in their house rather than in the basement cafeteria with the men, until they saw how compatible we were. They even included me in their family Bible reading and prayer time.

Now I began in earnest to have a deeper interest in spiritual things. I desired a revolutionary change from the inside out. But I found the change I needed harder to effect than anticipated. I certainly couldn't change myself, and I knew it. And the program at the Mission wasn't a radical enough environment shift to give me the support I needed to reprogram myself.

At that time their method consisted of meeting with the men's basic needs: food, clothing and shelter and preaching to them. It was a little bit like ware-housing the men and hoping that in time the message got through. I needed something more. I needed basic discipline and structure in my life. The Mission system seemed to work fine for a great many of the other residents, but I was the first of an oncoming new breed. Most of these men were beyond retirement age or close to it. True, there was *Barberton Joe* who was only 46, but he was so much younger than the rest that everyone called him *The Kid*. I, being only 19 years old at the time, was the next down the ladder from him. Most of these men had once had a career and a family but lost it all through drink. I, however had never yet embarked on a career or thought of having a family. Most of these men had been church bred and shared a basic value system of right and wrong. By contrast I had rarely seen the inside of a church and for me everything about ethics was up for grabs.

I had taken myself out of my old environment but now I needed to get the old environment out of me. I realized that either God was going to do it or it wasn't going to be done at all.

During the holiday season that year I shared my feelings with Bruce. He came up with an answer.

"You need to spend a while in Bible College, Max," he said.

"You mean there's a whole college built around Bible study?" I asked.

"Well that and related subjects; and yes, there are great many such colleges across America. It's where preachers start their training. It's where I was when God called me to start this mission."

"That's the one I want to go to! The one you did. What is the daily routine like?"

"You would be living on college grounds. They have dormitories. And the program is much more regimented than here. You might almost say that it's militaristic. They have a specific time for meals, for classes and to be up in the morning and in bed at night with the lights out."

"So they have rules?"

Bruce thought he had lost me there.

"Well, yes Max. You know there have to be rules so that... ," he began to defend. I caught his concern.

"No, no. Don't take me wrong. That's exactly what I want! It's what I need; A strong outer structure to hold me up! Until I get my own internal structure developed I need discipline."

"Oh, well then, what did you ask?"

"Are there rules?"

"Are there rules? Rules are the fuel that those places run on. At least that's how it was at the one I attended. If discipline is what you want then that's the place for you," Bruce said.

"When can I go?" I asked.

"They start the next semester right after the New Year begins."

"Could I move into the dormitory before then so I can get a job to pay for the tuition?" I asked.

"You need to stay on the campus for the first while Max. I'll pay for at least your first semester."

"Really? You mean it?"

"Yes."

"Wow! I mean thanks. How can I ever repay you?"

"Just become all you can."

"So when can I go?"

"The question is where do you want to go? As I said there are a number of them across the country."

"I want to go to the one you were at when you got your call to start this mission."

"That one is a good choice because it's only an hour or so away. I'll take you over January 2nd. You'll have to fill out an application and see if they'll accept you."

After New Year's Day Bruce and I made the trip. I was granted an interview with Rev. LeRoy Adams, the college president. Bruce and I sat in front of his desk in his office.

"So tell me young man, why do you want to come to college here?" He addressed me.

"I need to get more discipline in my life. I need to get God into my life." I told him.

After discussing the matter at some length Brother Adams, for so they called him, decided that he had better get more input before making this decision; he did, after all, have to answer to the families of the students who were residing there, a good number of whom were enrolled in the high school located on the same property. I understood perfectly well that he couldn't just bring people in off the street and put them in with the others; he was operating a Bible College not a Reform School.

So the board of the college was called together for a session and to meet with me.

In less than an hour they had gathered, and after only a few minutes Bruce was summoned in before them. A few minutes more and I was myself called for.

Stepping into the small room that contained an almost wall–to–wall table I saw eight men sandwiched around it. Almost as soon as I entered the room Bruce said,

"These men want to know more about you Max. Tell them your story."

I started with my previous atheism, my introduction to the occult, the demon attacks, using the name of Jesus, reading the Bible, praying, telling everyone I knew about the power of Jesus' name, and my continued war with the demons.

The board members started asking me questions about my personal life. Toward the end of the meeting one of them wanted to know,

"How long have you had victory over cigarettes?"

That was a perfectly legitimate question.

"Since last summer!" I lied. I was dying for one right then. I was desperate and I knew by how the meeting was going that if I told them the truth I would never get in. I needed this environment. I knew that the one book of the Bible I had studied–Revelation, told me where all liars go; hell. But I was convinced that I was already on my way there anyway so what harm could one more lie do? What did I have to lose? Where was I going to go? Hell number two? Hell number three?

I'll straighten this out after I get the help I need, I justified myself.

Soon the chairman of the board began to draw the meeting to a close. "You two can step out of the room while we make our decision." He said.

In a few minutes, we were called back in before the board and informed that I would be accepted on probation should I decide to stay. I did.

After saying goodbye to Bruce someone was appointed to show me to my quarters. It was a room for one in a separate building removed from the boy's dorm. To keep me safe from the others, I am sure. It was situated in a smaller barn shaped building, overtop a couple of classrooms. And while small and much longer than wide, it was comfortable enough. There was a door at one end that nearly took up the entire wall and a window overtop a steam radiator at the other. Through the window was a beautiful view of the pond with the building that housed Brother Adam's quarters just beyond it. The pond was frozen and with the students skating on it the scene lacked nothing that would be found in a Currier and Ives winter lithograph. The room was furnished with a mirrored antique dresser, an antique floor lamp, and a rather uncomfortable antique chair. A single bed lined the wall opposite the dresser. It sagged so bad in the center that it was impossible to sleep on except on your back, your arms straight down at your sides with your legs together as if you were on your feet standing at attention. With these few simple furnishings, the room was more than full. The shower and bathroom were down the hall.

I finished unpacking in time to find my way to the dining hall for dinner.

I started classes the next day but didn't do very well with my studies. Aside from not having developed actual study habits, I was too busy trying to get my life together to focus on much of anything else. I spent most of my time seeking God through prayer and Bible study and soon added fasting to my catalogue of weapons. I quickly became known as one of the most spiritual people on campus. Scary thought! Before long many of the students were coming to me for spiritual counsel and guidance. If the staff or board members knew a fraction of what I discovered from my sessions with the other students, they would have probably closed the place down or died from shock. Here as everywhere else I found that not all that glitters is gold.

Come Spring the college sponsored a series of meetings with an evangelist. I was surprised to see that it was somebody I already knew. We had met in my travels with Bruce. Mark Russell was the first man other than Bruce and Ron who had ever shown an honest concern for my soul.

One night during the Spring Revival I went forward to seek my peace with God. While praying at the alter it seemed that I was suddenly transported into eternity. I saw all history spread out before me in panoramic view. Creation was at the beginning and the Second Coming of Jesus at the end. In the middle I saw the cross with Jesus hanging on it. Instead of His blood flowing down I saw it flowing up and out of the time flow of history. When it hit eternity above the cross I saw it flowing backwards as far as creation and forward as far as the Second Coming. I knew that I was seeing the sufficiency of Jesus' blood to cleanse anyone's sins from wherever they were in time. That included me, my sins, and right then. I made up my mind on the spot that if God loved me enough to put that kind of effort into my salvation then I was going to seek it until I knew I had found it.

I immediately rose from the altar and looked up Brother Adams. I told him that I wanted to meet with the school board.

"Why is that?" he asked.

"I have to confess something to them," I said.

"And what would that be?" he probed further.

"I lied about smoking and a few other things to get into this college," I confessed. "It was wrong and I need to make it right. They can kick me out if they need to, I believe am ready to go now if I have to."

"You did the right thing to confess your wrong," he said, "but I'll tell them for you. If anything further is needed we will contact you."

"Are you sure," I asked.

"Yes, timing is everything on an issue like this. I will choose the right time to let them know."

I thanked him for his kind-hearted act of charity. I had always thought Brother Adams would prove to be a friend in the end, and indeed he did. I don't know how he handled it, but it worked. I never heard another thing about it.

Now that I had begun to grasp and pursue salvation in earnest I started to experience terrible depression. I believe it was one of the last weapons the enemy had in his arsenal to use on me.

Meanwhile back at the mission Bruce and Phyllis had been fasting and carrying a heavy burden in prayer for my friends and I. They would travel every weekend from Thursday or Friday, through Sunday representing the mission in various churches. On those days they would eat. But every Monday through Wednesday at least and sometimes through Thursday, 3 or 4 days out of every 7 they were fasting for my friends and I. Bruce's was a complete fast while Phyllis would fast either one meal a day or one day a week. This went on for 6 months that I know of. Someone later told me that during those days of intercession Bruce had confided in them,

"I couldn't love Max any more if he was my own flesh and blood."

No wonder he was an effective soul winner.

Bruce got an opportunity to add counsel to his prayers while I was on a home visit one weekend. I shared with him the struggles I had been having in my pursuit for peace.

"I have been going through terrible depression," I told him.

"Tell me about It," he encouraged.

"It's like I'm losing my mind Bruce. It's as if I am beside myself," I explained. He thought for a moment then said,

"There was someone in the Bible who was beside themselves–but Jesus fixed their problem."

"Who was that?" I asked, surprised that the Bible would be that up to date.

"He's called the prodigal son. You find the story in Luke chapter 15."

"How do you know he was beside himself?"

He grabbed a nearby Bible and opened it to Luke chapter 15. Finding the verse, he pointed at it and said,

"Here, read it for yourself. right there–verse 17."

I took the Bible and began to read aloud,

"And when he came to himself . . ."

"That's enough," Bruce said cutting me off. "You see when his life blew up in his face because of choices he had been making, it says–he *came to himself.*"

"So?"

"You can't come to yourself if you're not beside yourself," He explained.

"I think I understand." I said in a somewhat puzzled voice.

"Look. You told me that the army said you were simple schizophrenic, right?"

"Yes."

"I'm convinced that simple schizophrenia is nothing but an identity crises. You've just been trying to figure out who you are. Christ can set you free so you can find yourself and be yourself."

I found myself slowly shaking my head in agreement unconsciously. He continued,

"And as for losing your mind the Bible talks about another man who had lost his mind, but he found it."

"Tell me!" I said, finally feeling like I was getting somewhere.

"He was suffering depression too. The Bible says he was living in a graveyard and running around naked, crying and cutting himself."

"I can identify." I said.

"Well he was so miserable that he attacked anyone who came near to him."

"I relate to that kind of rage as well. And what does it say happened to him?"

"Well they would come out in mobs to subdue him and bind him in chains. But a rage would come on him and he would become so strong that he would break the chains and chase them off. But then he ran into Jesus who cast out the spirits that was in him," Bruce continued "and it says that when the people of the town came out to see Jesus they found this man . . . well here, let me find it and you can read it for yourself."

He flipped the Bible back a few pages and found the place in Luke 8. Again, handing it over to me with his finger pointing at verse 35, he instructed me to read.

"*Then they went out to see what was done; and came to Jesus, and found the man, out of whom the devils were departed, sitting at the feet of Jesus, clothed, and in his right mind: and they were afraid."*

Bruce said, "You see three things there. One, he was calmly sitting–he had been full of discontent and restlessness before. Two, he was clothed whereas he had previously been running among the tombs naked. And three, he was in his *right mind.*"

"Why does it say the people were afraid?" I wondered.

"Because people are always afraid of what they don't understand and they don't understand the kind of change Jesus makes in people when He gets a chance," Bruce answered.

"What became of him after that?" I inquired.

"He wanted to follow Jesus but Jesus told him to go back home and show his family, friends, and neighbors the great things God had done for him."

"So when people say you've gone off the deep end over religion, like some of my family has, they're wrong?" I quarried.

"Not really. A lot of people do lose their mind over religion. But no one has ever lost their mind over salvation."

"There's a difference?"

"Yes. Religion is when someone is trying to reach up to God. It's made up of liturgies, rituals, formulas, ceremonies and the like."

"OK," I said.

"Salvation is when God reaches down and gets hold of a person. It has nothing to do with our efforts other than repenting and believing."

"So a relationship with Christ is never going to mess with your mind?"

"No. In fact let me show you one more scripture. It's over here," he began flipping pages again. "In Paul's Letters. Look here at what it says."

Without being instructed this time, I took the Bible and began to read 2 Timothy 1:7,

"For God has not given us the Spirit of fear, but of power and of love and of a sound mind."

"You see there?" Bruce announced, "It is Christ's Spirit that gives you a sound mind."

"So, you're saying that the best thing I can do for my condition is to get more of the Spirit of God into my life?"

"That is certainly where it all starts. If you still have problems after that then we'll seek professional help, but not before then."

I carried that in my mind for the next several weeks. Then on a Friday evening, in one swift moment, God poured out all the bottled-up prayers and fasting that Bruce and Phyllis and others had been sending to heaven for me.

That night I attended a meeting a few miles down the road from the mission, in one of the churches that supported them. The service had just started when I arrived. The place was full so I had to march down the aisle for a seat about three rows from the front. They were already standing and singing so I took a song-book from its place and joined in.

Then the presence that I had come to recognize as the Spirit of God came into the building and it being one of those places where the Christians weren't afraid to say *Amen* right out load, they began to express their joy at the Lord's nearness. A strange thing happened that night. The happier the Christians got, the more miserable I became. What was this? We were both in God's presence but it was having two totally different effects on us.

Then I remembered that I had read in the Bible about the day of Pentecost when the Holy Spirit came upon the church for the first time. How the Christians praised God and everyone else was "*pricked in their consciences.*"

Is that what's happening here? I wondered. *Am I being pricked in my conscience?*

As we continued singing that inner voice I had come to know as God's, spoke to me.

"You need to go to the altar and make a public commitment to me." It said.

What? Right here? Right now, In front of all these people? What will they think of me?

"If you're ashamed of me . . ."

Yeah, yeah . . . I know.

"Then make the commitment."

But this isn't the time. It's inappropriate. Brother Adams said 'timing is everything.' They aren't trying to get anybody to make a commitment. They're just singing songs.

But I wasn't singing anymore. I had already slipped the songbook back into the rack. The voice spoke again.

"Anytime I say to do something is the right time. And I'm telling you that now is the time. If you will offer yourself to me tonight I will accept your offer and make the change in you that you have been searching for."

Something welled up within me and I said,

NO! I'm not going up there in front of all these people under these circumstances and make a fool out of myself!

"OK!" the voice seemed to say "If that's how you want it."

Right then I felt as if God took his hand off of me. It was as if hell had opened up and swallowed me alive. I thought I must have crossed some kind of deadline and grieved God right out of my life. I began to shake and tremble. I looked down at my knuckles. They were gripping the back of the pew so hard they were white.

I felt beads of perspiration standing out on my forehead. Others standing around me were completely oblivious to everything that was going on right beside them.

I'm getting out of here! I told myself.

I turned around and looked at the back door. It seemed to be a lot farther away than it had been when I first took my place in that pew. I was about to make a run for it when that inner voice spoke again.

"You've already tried everything out there Max. None of it gave you the peace you've been looking for. Why not give me an honest chance?"

But I don't want to make a spectacle out of myself by going up there in the middle of a song service, I told the voice. *I'm leaving!*

"How about if I make a spectacle out of you by striking you down in the aisle when you try?"

I decided to forget it. It wasn't worth taking the chance. I turned back around.

If you want me to give you an honest chance I will. But we can settle this later: after church!

"You're not the one making the conditions here. This is where it starts Max. It starts with obedience even when you don't understand why. Until you get to where you can't wait, you aren't where you need to be."

Now the altar seemed to have grown in size. It was all that I could see.

I wish I was dead! I declared to the voice.

"Do you know that your sins are forgiven?"

No. How could I be when I'm disobeying you at this very moment? I frankly told it.

"Then you aren't ready to die. If you died in disobedience you'd end up in hell," the voice said. I felt like I was there already.

Now I was afraid to even think.

What was this voice trying to do? Work me into a corner or something?

"Exactly!" the voice that I now wasn't even talking to said, "That's what I had to do with the prodigal son. And it's what I have to do with most people."

That was it! I had had enough! I broke out from behind my pew and headed straight for the altar. I wasn't going to give the devil or myself any more time to talk me out of this. And I couldn't help it if I broke up their song service. I had eternal business to take care of. Preaching would have to wait. For now, anything other than obedience was simply playing church.

I threw myself across the altar and began praying like the place was on fire. In fact I was praying like all hell was on fire and I was in it, because as far as I could see I was as good as there. I was pretty sure that I had likely sinned away my day of grace.

My prayer was neither dignified nor refined. I was much too desperate for that. I nearly screamed,

"Oh God! I'll do anything if you'll just save me!"

I didn't know what to expect but I didn't pray that way long before something happened. I felt a huge burden roll off me. I hadn't even realized that it was there. I suppose that's because I had become so accustomed to it. I felt guilt and condemnation lift off of my soul and the warmth of God's peace and love come flowing into my heart in its place. I could no longer pray about being forgiven after that. It was futile to ask for what had already been so clearly given.

When I looked up the entire altar was lined with people from one end to the other. Apparently, God had been speaking to a lot of others that night, but it took someone obeying Him to break the devil's hold on the atmosphere. Though I did not realize it, I had apparently walked into the service that night carrying the keys to it with me. I think in most church gatherings somebody present has the keys to it. And I have found since that day that obedience is the best way in the world to bring the glory, power and conviction of God on the scene.

When most of the others had stopped praying someone suggested that I stand and tell what Jesus had done for me. I rose to my feet and said,

"I'm not sure if this is what they call being saved or not. But I'll tell you this much—something revolutionary has happened inside of me tonight."

That brought a great many *Amens* and *Praise the Lords* from those around.

As I stood by the altar I felt as light as a feather: as if I could float down the aisle and on out the door. I had an inner assurance that everything was well between God and me. The thought of dying did not alarm me in the least any longer. I didn't need to fear. I was sure that if I died on the spot I was ready to meet God. In fact I wondered if I weren't half way to heaven already. I felt so free; free from guilt, and free from confusion. Everything felt so different. This didn't seem like the old me I had known for so long. *I had come to myself.*

I later read Dwight L. Moody's testimony about how his Sunday School teacher visited him in the Boston cobbler shop where he worked. After the teacher had led him in a prayer of confession and repentance Dwight went out into Boston Commons to eat his lunch where he declared that the sky seemed bluer, the grass looked greener, and birds sang sweeter than they ever had before.

My story isn't the same. I couldn't see the sky or grass when we stepped out of the church that night, because it was dark. The birds were all asleep in their nests. But the air did seem especially crisp and fresh and when we stopped at a hamburger shop on the way home, as I sat waiting for my order I remember noticing how the white tiles on the floor and walls just glistened. They seemed to glow as if there was a neon light shining through them. I took it as a kind of confirmation from the Lord that He had indeed accepted me as His own. *I had come to myself.*

For years, I had experienced extreme emotional confusion. But that night was the beginning of life starting to make sense as the pieces of the puzzle began to fall into place. It was from that night forward that the darkness began to lift, the fog to dissipate, the clouds to part, and the sun to come breaking through. That was the point from which everything began to come into focus until life became crystal clear! *I had come to myself.*

It wasn't automatic though for I had to begin doing those things that I knew would feed this new nature or whatever it was that I had. I began to establish the daily habit of praying and studying the Bible. Following Emil Matson's pattern, I literally began reprogramming my mind according to the thought patterns of the scripture by memorizing as large tracts of it as I was capable of. It worked! I began to view life from a Christian perspective as the scriptures got down into a functional level in my soul. Bruce was right. *I had come to myself!*

CHAPTER 10

THE VOID

I may not have been sure that what happened at the alter the night I went forward was what they called being born again, but the further I have walked away from the experience the more convinced I have become that God for Jesus sake did indeed forgive my sins that night.

I found it hard to believe that someone as insignificant as myself down here on the edge of the twentieth century had found that which all mankind has been searching for throughout the endless ages of time. To offer it to someone was like offering him or her a million dollars. It still is.

I left college at the end of that semester and began traveling, telling anyone I could get to listen, how I had found the peace for which all mankind is searching.

Soon I was married and pastoring my first church while still traveling extensively. Then many of my family members began also giving their lives to the Lord; mother, father, stepfather, brother, aunts, uncles, and cousins. By now most of them have died in the faith. You can read the continuing story of God sweeping through the ranks of our family in book three of the *Believe It or Not Series* entitled, "*And Your House.*" The first book in the series "*The Gates of Hell*" takes a closer look at my experiences in the occult with a special emphasis toward convincing unbelievers of spiritual realities.

Fourteen years after my conversion I returned to the Barberton Rescue Mission to work, first as a counselor, then as the co–director. By then over half of the men in the program were under thirty-five years of age and most of them were exactly like I had been when I first arrived. Today, Bruce having passed away and new management having come in, the programming has changed to meet the needs of the *new breed*. Operating under the name *New Destiny Treatment Center* the rescue mission has become a full-fledged substance abuse rehabilitation facility with a nine-month program. I did a second stint working there under the new administration as a therapist for a number of years. The last I knew New Destiny was the largest licensed rehabilitation facility in the state of Ohio and I believe they still maintain the highest success rate in the state. A couple of my nieces work and minister there to this day.

Throughout my ministry, which is approaching 50 years now, I have pastored six churches, served as associate in two others, held an untold number of revivals, preached on street corners, ministered in bars, shared my faith on various secular college campuses, conducted seminars, wrote books and articles, done artwork, administrated in various parachurch organizations, served as a school principal, taught high school, lead choir, done social work, counseled alcoholics, drug addicts, troubled teens, prisoners, and married couples in a variety of ministry settings, been involved in one capacity or the other in the starting of nearly a dozen churches, traveled to 11 countries in behalf of the gospel, ministered on several mission fields and been involved in just about any ministerial effort you could imagine.

Since the day I began preaching I have never had a free Sunday unless I took it off on purpose and I still have more places to minister than I can get to.

I praise God for my wife and for the life He has blessed us with.

If I were to sum my testimony up in a few words, it would be the same as the wise man in the Biblical book of *Ecclesiastes*. He declares six times in his little volume, that everything is meaningless at best; a chasing after and feeding upon the wind, and a vexation of the spirit at worse; nothing but a burden to the essential you.; everything that is, except to serve and worship God and obey His commandments—the Old Testament equivalent of being born again.

I can't express it any better; everything is a burden to the soul except to serve Jesus. I have found it to be so. The reason is easy to explain.

According to the Bible man was made in the image of God (Gen. 1:27) but when he sinned and fell from grace he lost that image. When he started having children they were born in his own image (Gen. 5:3), which was now a fallen image rather than God's. Every individual that has ever been born into Adam's race from that day to this has been born with a void, a vacuum, an emptiness within where the image of God used to be (Ps. 51:5). That is why you must teach children to do good but no one needs to show them how to do wrong; that will come automatically (Ps. 58:3).

Everyone feels *the emptiness* within and seeks to fill it. But since the emptiness is shaped exactly like Jesus Christ, to try and fill it with anything other than Him is like trying to force the proverbial square peg into a round hole; it just doesn't fit!

My own personal experience corroborates this. From my youngest days I felt something lacking within despite knowing nearly nothing about spiritual things. No one in our family went to church, read the Bible, prayed, or talked about spiritual matters. Still I was aware of an *emptiness* I could not explain. I instinctively knew something was missing. I felt it and I sought to fill it.

Since we are physical beings living in a material world, when we feel *the emptiness* within we begin our search, consciously or otherwise, among those things we know best: the material, physical things that surround us. Sometimes we never seem to catch on that the tangible things of time, though deposited by the dump truck load into the abyss will never fill this internal gaping cavity.

Then there are rarer souls every now and again who seem to catch on rather quickly that these things aren't going to satisfy, and so widen their search to include less tangible and more spiritual options. That is when we pray that, by the providence of God, some Christian soul will be there and that God will open a door for them to provide guidance. Otherwise a great many of these will find themselves caught up in some cult or ism, which worsens their condition because they think they have found something worthwhile when in fact, what they have actually discovered is something infinitely worse than nothing. What they have found is at best a deceptive, cheap and deadly imitation of the true object of their quest (Matt. 23:15).

I am not suggesting that everyone is conscious that this is going on inside of them. Nevertheless, as a person doesn't have to intellectually understand diseases to know when they are afflicted with one, it is also true that the unconverted, though not instructed in spiritual matters are on some level aware that something is not quite right inside of them. As may be the case with physical sicknesses, so a non-Christian may not know wherein the problem lies, its name, how it is classified, where it came from, the cure or even if there is one, to know something is wrong. They know it by the symptoms; in the case of a physical illness it is by the headache, the fever, the aching body and nausea; in matters of the spirit it is by the restlessness, discontent and the continual quest for something more or better put; something else.

It takes a level of optimism bordering on the absurd to deny that mankind has a universal problem. Just skim the closest textbook on history, or this evening's newspaper or listen to the next news broadcast and you will be forced to acknowledge that man outside of Christ is diabolically wicked and capable of absolutely anything. Sin is a reality. So much so that it constitutes one of the greatest trials to our faith.

I am also glad that we don't have to understand the spiritual disease with which our race is afflicted or its cure before the cure will work. If a soul will but give the remedy set forth in the scriptures an honest chance they will discover it to be more than they could have hoped for. In my early days as a Christian I often declared that what had befallen me was "just too good to be true." And yet it *was* and still *is* true. I have often wished that I could take what I experience in my inner person and place it inside the seeking soul for only a moment so they could know what it is like. If I could do this, I believe they would become a Christian forever. But no one need take my word for it, "*taste and see that the Lord is good!*" (Psalm 34:8) There is nothing to be lost because it is for sure that the devil will always be glad to take any dissatisfied soul back!

To continue with our analogy between sin and sickness let's suppose that an aborigine in the jungles of the outback gets sick, but some of his fellow tribesmen tell him that they know what ails him because they too were afflicted with the same condition. He knows what they are saying is true because he has seen them in their sick state but now sees that they are well.

So, he asks how they got better, for he has seen others die from the same disorder, which has led him to conclude that if left unaddressed his illness is terminal. They confirm his worse suspicions that the disease will not get better on its own but then they also inform him that a specific application of a particular cure will free him of his ailment.

They tell him that there is a missionary in a neighboring village who has a medicine that will heal his sickness. Let's suppose that this sick man is persuaded by his friends' testimonies and their changed lives to stagger his way down the jungle trail to the next village and look up the missionary's clinic, what do you predict will happen.

Do you think that the missionary will teach the poor man how to read and then give him an encyclopedia on medicine so he can understand the source and history of his sickness and how it is spread? Will he then give him biology classes on the various types of cures people have tried and then finally isolate the one that is actually effective and explain in detail why and how it works; where the medicine comes from, how it is chemically processed, the different ways in which it can be administered and the biological effect it will have on his body's system?

Nonsense! All the missionary will do is give the man a shot in his arm and it will fix his problem. It is as simple as that. In the same way, a person doesn't have to know or understand everything about salvation before it will work.

Like one fellow said, "I don't understand how these lights work but I'm sure not going to sit here in the dark and try to figure it out." Let's be practical; take advantage of the fact that the lights DO work. Turn them on! Then if you are one of those inquisitive souls who are inclined in such a way as to dissect the light bulb into its various components and attempt to arrive

at a deeper understanding of how it works its magic–
go ahead!

On the spiritual level let the Lord flip the light of grace on in your heart. Take advantage of the fact that salvation does work. Then if you are inquisitive enough, go get some books on theology and try to figure out all the whys and wherefores. In fact, go get a doctorate in theology if you so desire. But surely don't wait until you get it all figured out before you avail yourself of God's grace! For if you do it is certain you will die in your sin, because you are trying to understand something that is on a completely different level than you are thinking. When it comes to spiritual matters, *send your heart express and your brain freight!* Maybe the brain will catch up eventually, but if it doesn't it's no great loss. And to be honest I doubt that it ever will, for some of the greatest minds that have graced our planet have studied a lifetime and still never plummeted the depths of what God did for them the day or night He saved them. It is my firm conviction that none of us ever will understand it all until we get to heaven, and maybe not then.

If you feel a pull, a tug upon your heart or soul or inner person or however you want to identify it, as you read this, follow that drawing for it is "*the goodness of God* [leading] *you to repentance.*" (Rom 2:4) If you will follow that pull it will land you in the midst of the most wonderful and glorious experience with Jesus Christ you ever imagined possible.

Then find yourself a good body of believers, a church, and start attending. But know this, setting in a room with a bunch of people who are mostly strangers for an hour once a week is not going to suffice. Become active in that church. Get down into its fellowship level; the small groups–Sunday school, Bible studies, spiritual care groups or whatever they

221

have available, for it is there that you will get plugged into the flow of what God is doing in that setting, and it is there that the fellowship will be intimate enough to be meaningful.

Don't be unrealistic in your expectations but if you find that one church doesn't work for you, keep searching until you find one that does. Also, establish yourself in a Bible reading program and regular prayer life.

Now, if you haven't started on your journey yet, I invite you to join me in the greatest adventure known to man. It's as simple as ABC;

A–Admit that you need forgiveness
B–Be willing, with God's help, to turn from all sin as He reveals it to you and
C–Claim what Jesus did on the cross as payment for your sins.

If you will do these things I have every good reason to believe that I will meet you in heaven one day. Until then I leave you with this poem, written by a lady who once pastored my home church in Massillon, Ohio; Clare Teare Williams wrote:

All my lifelong I had panted
For a drink from some cool spring
That I hoped would quench the burning
Of the thirst I felt within

Feeding on the husk around me
Till my strength was almost gone
Longed my soul for something better
Only still to hunger on

Poor I was and sought for riches

Something that would satisfy
But the dust I gathered 'round me
Only mocked my soul's sad cry.

But I love the fourth verse for it is the answer to all of the others,

Well of water, ever springing
Bread of life so rich and free
Untold wealth that never faileth
My redeemer is to me

Hallelujah! I have found Him
Who my soul so long has craved
Jesus satisfies every longing
Through His blood, I now am saved!

This poem was set to music and can be found in many hymnals under the name *Satisfied*. Clare like myself found the object of *The Pursuit of Peace* in the one place it will ever and always be inevitably found: Jesus Christ!

If I can be of further help, email or write me at the addresses included at the end of this book.

Lastly, I invite you to read Books one and three of the *Believe It Or Not Series*; Book one: *The Gates of Hell* and *Book Three, And Your House.* can be found on Amazon.com.

Until we meet, here or on the other side, may God's peace be multiplied unto you!

THE END

ABOUT THE AUTHOR

Born in Chicago, Illinois, and raised primarily in Akron, Ohio, Max Wood spent years in a search for the purpose of life. His quest took him from street gangs, to the drug scene, and from a hippie lifestyle to playing in a rock and roll band. He became a political activist in the revolutionary movement of the 1960's to the point of involvement with the American Communist Party. Finally, he fell into the occult, which opened his eyes to the reality of a spirit world and eventually led him to the real meaning of life.

To request other materials, arrange for speaking engagements and seminars, or for consultation, you may contact Max at:

Council Publications
P.O. Box 1683
Elyria, Ohio 44036

or

CounselMinistries@yahoo.com

Also by the same author

The Gates of Hell
*An Atheist's Encounter with the Spirit World
and Where It Led Him*
And Your House
*Salvation is For the Family Not Just the
Individual*
The Drugs and Alcohol Primer
*The Christian's Introduction to the World of
Substance Abuse and Recovery*
Beyond the Smokescreen
*A 10 Day 12-Step Smoking Cessation Pro-
gram*
Rock and Roll an Analysis of the Music
*An Appeal for Readers To Be Aware of What
They Are Listening To.*

Available Soon . . .

What Is Your Name?
Know What to Do by Knowing Who You Are
Through the Beaded Curtain
An Autobiographic Novel
War in the Heavenlies
A Spiritual Warfare Commentary on Ephesians
The Survival Guide for the Spiritual Warrior
Hard-Learned Lessons in Spiritual Warfare

Made in the USA
Columbia, SC
18 June 2024